S·H·P
THE
SCHOOLS
HISTORY
PROJECT

DISCOVERING THE PAST

THE
RENAISSANCE

Rose Barling
Valerie Boyes
Series Editor: Colin Shephard (Director, SHP)

JOHN MURRAY

Acknowledgements

Illustrations by David Anstey, Art Construction, Peter Bull Art Studio

Photographs are reproduced by kind permission of:
cover *left* British Library, London; *right* The National Gallery, London/Bridgeman Art Library. **p.6** *top left* British Library/Bridgeman Art Library, London; *top right* Bodleian Library, Oxford, MS Ashmole 399, fo. 14r; *bottom right* Trinity College, Cambridge. **p.7** *top right* Mary Evans Picture Library; *centre right* The Royal Collection, © Her Majesty the Queen; *bottom* Fotomas Index. **p.10** *bottom* Scala. **p.12** Scala. **p.13** *top* Ronald Sheridan/Ancient Art and Architecture Collection. **p.14** *top left* Stanley Gibbons/Bridgeman Art Library; *centre left and right* Scala. **p.15** *top* Giraudon/Bridgeman Art Library; *left* Scala. **p.17** *left and top right* The Royal Collection, © Her Majesty the Queen; *centre and bottom right* Giraudon. **p.18** *top right* Paris, Bibliothèque de l'Institut de France/Giraudon; *bottom right* The Royal Collection, © Her Majesty the Queen. **p.19** *top right and centre left* Scala; *centre* The Royal Collection, © Her Majesty the Queen. **p.20** Mansell Collection. **pp.22–23** The National Gallery, London/Bridgeman Art Library. **p.23** *top right* British Library. **pp.24, 25** The National Gallery, London/Bridgeman Art Library. **p.26** *left* Winchester Cathedral/ Bridgeman Art Library; *right* The Trustees of the National Gallery, London. **p.27** The National Gallery, London/Bridgeman Art Library, London. **p.31** *top left and right* Staatliche Museen zu Berlin – Preußischer Kulturbesitz Gemäldegalerie; *bottom left and right* The National Gallery, London/Bridgeman Art Library, London. **p.32** *left* Staaatliche Museen zu Berlin – Kupferstichkabinett. **p.33** *centre* Roy Rainford/Robert Harding Picture Library. **p.34** *top* Scala; *centre* Grazia Neri/Camera Press; *bottom* Ray Roberts/Impact. **p.35** *top* Ancient Art and Architecture Collection. **p.36** *left* Archivi Alinari; *right* Alberto Bruschi di Grassina Collection, Florence/ Bridgeman Art Library, London. **p.37** Mansell Collection. **p.39** Southampton City Art Gallery. **p.40** Hulton Deutsch Collection. **p.43** *left* The Wellcome Institute Library, London; *right* Ann Ronan at Image Select. **p.44** *top* Mary Evans Picture Library; *bottom* Ann Ronan at Image Select. **p.47** Mary Evans Picture Library. **p.48** Ann Ronan at Image Select. **p.50** *right* Staatliche Museen zu Berlin – Gemäldegalerie; *left* Fitzwilliam Museum, University of Cambridge/Bridgeman Art Library, London. **p.51** *left* Kunsthistorisches Museum, Vienna; *right* The Royal Collection, © Her Majesty the Queen. **p.52** Fotomas Index. **p.53** Giraudon/Bridgeman Art Library. **p.54** *left* A.F. Kersting; *right* Trinity College, Cambridge. **p.56** Mary Evans Picture Library. **p.58** *right* British Library.

Pupils Book 0–7195–5186–2
Teachers' Evaluation Pack 0–7195–5187–0

© Rose Barling, Valerie Boyes 1995

First published in 1995
by John Murray (Publishers) Ltd
50 Albemarle Street, London W1X 4BD

Reprinted 1996

Layouts by Ann Samuel
Typeset by Wearset, Boldon, Tyne and Wear
Printed in Great Britain by Cambus Litho, East Kilbride

A CIP record for this book is available from the British Library
ISBN 0–7195–5186–2

The authors and publishers would also like to thank the following for permission to reproduce copyright material:
B.T. Batsford Ltd (Peter Burke, *The Italian Renaissance*); Ilinca R. Bossy (Vincent Cronin, *The Florentine Renaissance*); Doubleday, a division of Bantam Doubleday Dell Publishing Group, Inc. (Irving Stone, *The Agony and the Ecstasy*); Phaidon Press Ltd (Max J. Friedländer, *Van Eyck to Bruegel vol. 2*); Longman Group Ltd (E.R. Chamberlin, *Florence in the time of the Medici*).

Every effort has been made to trace all the copyright holders, but if any have been inadvertently overlooked the publishers will be pleased to make the necessary arrangement at the first opportunity.

Note: The wording and sentence structure of some written sources have been adapted and simplified to make them accessible to all pupils, while faithfully preserving the sense of the original.

THE SCHOOLS HISTORY PROJECT

This project was set up by the Schools Council in 1972. Its main aim was to suggest suitable objectives for history teachers, and to promote the use of appropriate materials and teaching methods for their realization. This involved a reconsideration of the nature of history and its relevance in secondary schools, the design of a syllabus framework which shows the uses of history in the teaching of adolescents, and the setting up of appropriate examinations.

Since 1978 the project has been based at Trinity and All Saints' College, Leeds. It is now self-funding and with the advent of the National Curriculum it has expanded its publications to provide courses throughout Key Stages 1–3, and for a range of GCSE and A level syllabuses. The project provides INSET for all aspects of National Curriculum, GCSE and A level history, and also publishes *Discoveries*, a twice-yearly journal for history teachers.

Enquiries about the project, INSET and *Discoveries* should be addressed to the Schools History Project, Trinity and All Saints' College, Brownberrie Lane, Horsforth, Leeds LS18 5HD.

Enquiries about the *Discovering the Past* series should be addressed to the publishers, John Murray.

Series consultants
Terry Fiehn
Tim Lomas
Martin and Jenny Tucker

Contents

Section 1   Introduction   6
             What was the Renaissance?   6

Section 2   What changed?   10
             Italy in the fifteenth century   10
             Leonardo da Vinci: a Renaissance man?   14
             How did art change?   22
             How did a Renaissance artist work?   28
             A Renaissance portrait gallery   30
             A tour through Florence: how did architecture
                 change?   32
             What was the role of women during the
                 Renaissance?   36
             Did health and medicine improve?   40
             Was the Earth the centre of the universe?   46

Section 3   How and why did the Renaissance spread?   50
             Was there a Renaissance in other parts of
                 Europe?   50
             Would the Renaissance have spread without the
                 printing press?   54
             Why did the Renaissance start in Italy?   60

Section 4   Conclusion   62
             What has the Renaissance given us?   62

Glossary   63

Index   64

N.B. Words in SMALL CAPITALS are defined in the glossary on page 63.

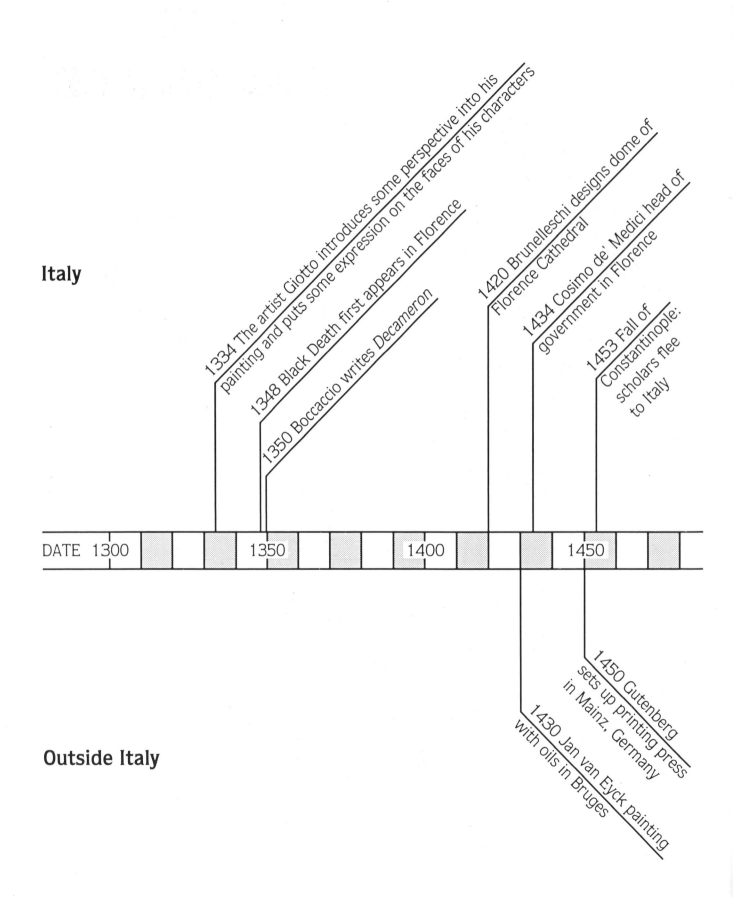

Italy

1334 The artist Giotto introduces some perspective into his painting and puts some expression on the faces of his characters

1348 Black Death first appears in Florence

1350 Boccaccio writes *Decameron*

1420 Brunelleschi designs dome of Florence Cathedral

1434 Cosimo de' Medici head of government in Florence

1453 Fall of Constantinople: scholars flee to Italy

DATE 1300   1350   1400   1450

Outside Italy

1450 Gutenberg sets up printing press in Mainz, Germany

1430 Jan van Eyck painting with oils in Bruges

THE RENAISSANCE

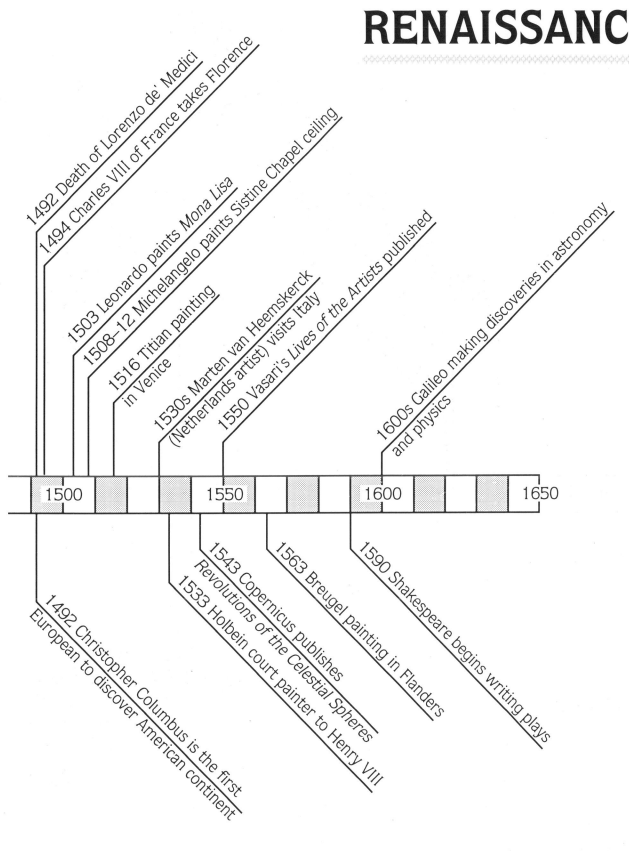

1492 Death of Lorenzo de' Medici

1494 Charles VIII of France takes Florence

1503 Leonardo paints Mona Lisa

1508–12 Michelangelo paints Sistine Chapel ceiling

1516 Titian painting in Venice

1530s Marten van Heemskerck (Netherlands artist) visits Italy

1550 Vasari's Lives of the Artists published

1600s Galileo making discoveries in astronomy and physics

1500

1550

1600

1650

1492 Christopher Columbus is the first European to discover American continent

1533 Holbein court painter to Henry VIII

1543 Copernicus publishes Revolutions of the Celestial Spheres

1563 Breugel painting in Flanders

1590 Shakespeare begins writing plays

What was the Renaissance?

Medieval Europe

Sources 1–4 were made between 1000 and 1400, or show what people of the Middle Ages believed.

SOURCE 1 A map of the world, made in the fourteenth century

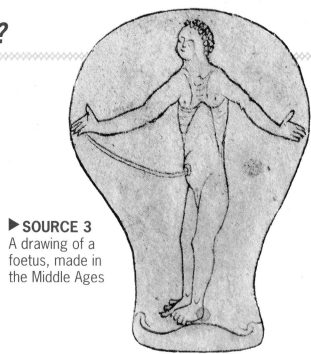

▶ SOURCE 3 A drawing of a foetus, made in the Middle Ages

▼ SOURCE 2 The medieval view of the universe

The Sun and the planets orbit around the Earth, which is at the centre of the whole universe

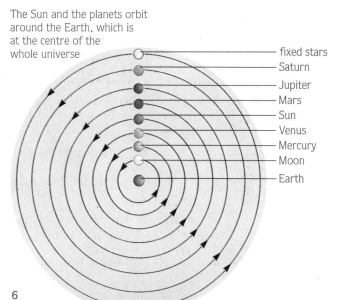

- fixed stars
- Saturn
- Jupiter
- Mars
- Sun
- Venus
- Mercury
- Moon
- Earth

SOURCE 4 A monk producing a handwritten book. All books were made this way in the Middle Ages

Renaissance Europe

Sources 5–8 were made between 1400 and 1600, or show what people of the Renaissance period believed.

▶ **SOURCE 6** Printers making a book

▼**SOURCE 5** The Renaissance view of the universe

The Sun is at the centre. The Earth and the other planets orbit around it

- fixed stars
- Saturn
- Jupiter
- Mars
- Moon
- Earth
- Venus
- Mercury
- Sun

▶ **SOURCE 7** A drawing of a foetus, made by Leonardo da Vinci in 1510

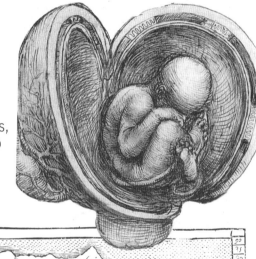

▲**SOURCE 8** A map of the world, made in 1527

1. Match the Renaissance pictures (Sources 5–8) to the medieval pictures (Sources 1–4) which show the same subject.
2. Take one pair and describe the differences and similarities between the medieval picture and the Renaissance picture.

WHAT WAS THE RENAISSANCE?

The changes shown by Sources 1–8 on the previous pages are just some of those that took place during the Renaissance. Art and architecture changed as artists developed new interests and new skills. Science changed – people's knowledge of the world and of the universe increased dramatically. Medicine changed as people improved their understanding of the body. But more importantly, many people's attitudes and beliefs changed as well, as you can see in Source 9.

'Rebirth'

Renaissance is a French word. It means 'rebirth'. It's a strange name for a period of history. What was it that was 'reborn' during the Renaissance?

To answer this question we need to look back at a much earlier period of history – the time of the Roman Empire. At this time Roman artists, scientists and writers influenced by Greek ideas were the world's most advanced. They had become skilled observers of the natural world around them, and had become experts in studying animals, plants, the human body or the stars and planets. They wrote down their ideas about what they saw, and based their theories about the world on their observations.

During the fourth and fifth centuries the Roman Empire slowly collapsed. War and disorder gradually spread through Italy and Europe. Many of the Romans' fine buildings, art and sculptures were destroyed. Some of their MANUSCRIPTS were lost as well. But most importantly, some of the ancient attitudes were lost. A questioning approach to the world was replaced by an unquestioning one.

Why did this happen? One reason was to do with the influence of the Christian Church. Through the

SOURCE 9 The Renaissance way of thinking

thousand years following the fall of the Roman Empire, the Church was the only strong organisation to survive. As you will know from your study of the Middle Ages, the Church controlled many aspects of life. In particular it controlled education and learning, and ran all the universities. The Church thought that the aim of a university should be to teach old ideas more clearly, not to introduce new ones. The scholars in the universities were nearly all priests. They were expected to study God and heaven from the Bible and ancient books, rather than the world around them.

Take medicine, for example. The main textbook for doctors had been written by a Greek doctor called Galen more than a thousand years earlier. But when Roger Bacon, a thirteenth-century priest, said that a new approach to medicine was needed – doctors should do their own original research instead of reading writers from the past such as Galen – the Church put him in prison.

By the time of the fourteenth century, however, some parts of the Christian Church were becoming less rigid in their ideas. As you can see from Source 9, there was a new state of mind among artists, doctors and scientists. People wanted to find out more about the world by studying it. This attitude of enquiry had been common in classical scholars, and it was 'reborn' during the Renaissance.

Where and when did it happen?

The Renaissance began in the towns of Italy, and spread later to other parts of Europe (see Source 10). This happened roughly between 1300 and 1600. But the Renaissance is not an event like someone's birth. Things did not change overnight, so it is difficult to give dates for when it started and finished. The rebirth of interest in the natural world and in the ideas of the Greeks and Romans began during the Middle Ages, and the changes which followed were very slow and gradual, and took place at different rates in different places. The periods of the Middle Ages and the Renaissance therefore overlap.

In this book we will be asking two main questions about the Renaissance:

■ How did the Renaissance change Italy and other parts of Europe?

■ Why did this rebirth happen where it did and when it did?

These are difficult questions. Historians don't agree about the answers, and this book will help you to see why there is disagreement, and to make up your own mind.

1. Match up the heads and tails of the following sentences:

   Heads

   The word Renaissance
   There was a rebirth of interest in the ideas
   In the Middle Ages
   These changes happened

   Tails

   people believed that reading the Bible was the best way to understand the world.
   between 1300 and 1600.
   means 'rebirth'.
   of the classical Greeks and Romans.

2. Use the information on the last four pages to write two more sentences which give us an important piece of information about the Renaissance.

3. Draw a timeline from 2000 BC to AD 2000. A scale of 10 cm = 500 years is a good one to use. Mark on it the following historical periods (all the dates are rough):
   The Roman Empire (400 BC to AD 400)
   The Renaissance (AD 1300 to AD 1600)
   The Middle Ages (AD 400 to AD 1400)
   Ancient Greece (1400 BC to 300 BC)

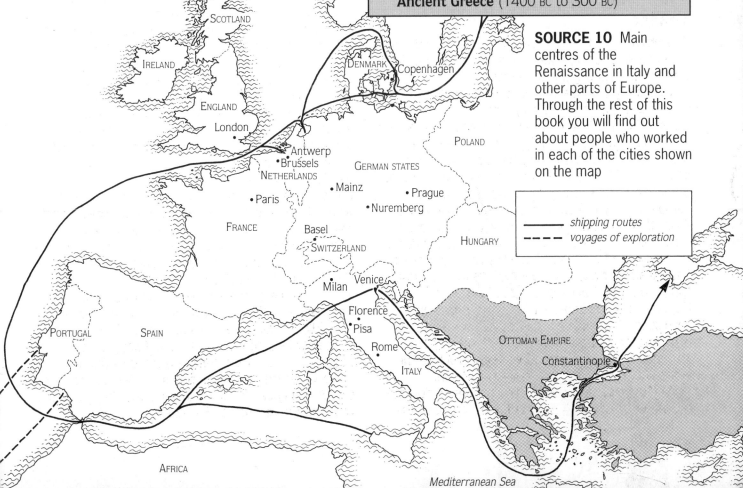

SOURCE 10 Main centres of the Renaissance in Italy and other parts of Europe. Through the rest of this book you will find out about people who worked in each of the cities shown on the map

——	shipping routes
- - -	voyages of exploration

Italy in the fifteenth century

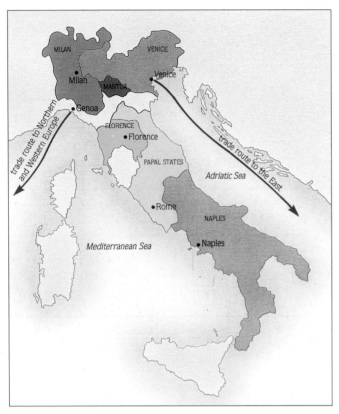

▲SOURCE 1 Italy and its city states

THE Renaissance began in Italy. What was Italy like in the fifteenth century, and how was it changing?

City States

As you can see from Source 1, in the fifteenth century Italy had no single ruler. Instead it was a collection of independent states, known as 'city states' because each one was run by a central city such as Florence. Some were small, some were large. Most states had their own government, laws and money. The most important were Florence, Venice, Milan, Naples and the Papal States around Rome (ruled by the Pope). During the Middle Ages these five city states had also become very rich and very powerful. Venice became rich from its trade with the Far East, the Mediterranean and the rest of Europe. Florence made its money from its cloth trade and banking. Banks in Florence lent money to businesses and governments all over Europe.

The people of each state thought of themselves as Florentines or Venetians, not as Italians. There was great rivalry between the city states – which led to regular wars – and between the families which ruled them.

The city states also competed with each other to build the grandest or tallest buildings (see Sources 4 and 5). They were prepared to pay a lot of money to attract the cleverest and most skilful artists to their city.

Let's look in detail at one city – Florence. Source 2 gives you a view over Florence towards the end of the fifteenth century.

▼SOURCE 2 Florence. Painted in about 1490

FIORENZA

In 1400 Florence was one of the largest cities in Italy. Between 60,000 and 100,000 people lived there – twice as many as lived in London at that time.

Florence was the centre of a rich trade in wool and cloth. In the area around the city there were 270 woollen mills and 83 factories producing expensive materials such as silk, BROCADE and DAMASK, which were much in demand among rich people all over Europe. One-third of the workers in Florence worked in the wool trade.

Most of Tuscany – the hilly farming area all around the city – was also owned or controlled by Florence's businessmen.

The most powerful family in Florence was the Medici family, who had made their money through banking. The most famous member of the family was Lorenzo de' Medici who ruled the city between 1469 and 1492.

The other powerful people who had influence in Florence were the members of the GUILDS. Craftsmen such as goldsmiths, artists, weavers or carpenters each had their own guild. There was even a butchers' guild. If you were a member of a guild and over 25 years old then you could be involved in governing the city.

The rulers of Florence wanted their city to be impressive and famous. The Medici collected books and built a huge library to house them. They spent money on renovating old buildings and putting up new ones. They restored churches, monasteries and CONVENTS, and set up an orphanage called the Hospital for the Innocents. They built a magnificent palace and employed painters and sculptors to decorate it. Some of the best and most famous artists were brought to work in Florence.

SOURCE 3 Fifteenth-century Florence. List all the different activities you can see taking place

SOURCE 4 Written by the CHANCELLOR of Florence in around 1400

What city, not merely in Italy but in the whole world, is stronger within its circle of walls, prouder in palaces, richer in temples, more lovely in buildings?

SOURCE 5 Written by a Florentine merchant in a letter to a friend in Venice

Florence is more beautiful and five hundred and forty years older than your Venice. We spring from very noble families . . . We have round about us thirty thousand estates . . . We have two trades greater than any four of yours in Venice put together.

1. On your own copy of Source 1 colour in the areas controlled by the main city states. Then mark on the map the names of the ruling families, which are listed below.

State	Ruler
Florence	Medici family
Milan	Sforza family
Papal States	The Pope
Venice	The Doge
Mantua	Gonzaga family
Naples	The King of Aragon (in Spain)

2. Look at Sources 4 and 5. In what ways do the writers think Florence is superior to other cities?

Activity

Design the front page of a fifteenth-century tourist brochure to attract visitors to Florence.

ITALY IN THE FIFTEENTH CENTURY

Towns

As well as the big cities such as Florence, Italy had more large towns than the rest of Europe put together. It was the most URBANISED area in Europe, with ten per cent of the population living in towns.

These towns raised money by taxing all goods brought into them. Among the people who lived there were merchants, professional men, craftsmen and shopkeepers.

Rich people liked living in towns because they were protected by walls and they felt safer than when they were out in the countryside, where they might be attacked by robbers or bands of hired soldiers. They had the money and the security to enjoy themselves.

The poor came to the towns because there was often better-paid work there than in the country, although towns were less healthy than the countryside and there was always a risk of being struck by diseases such as the plague.

War

Italian city states were constantly at war with their rivals, but the cities usually hired professional armies to fight their wars for them. Gone were the days when the city state expected ordinary, untrained citizens to go to war. Each major city had enough money to employ armies of professional soldiers, or mercenaries as we would call them. In the fourteenth century the wars between the states were no more than skirmishes. The aim was to raid opponents' property rather than to kill their soldiers. Battles involving thousands of soldiers could end with a handshake, without any casualties being incurred on either side.

In the fifteenth century, however, warfare became more serious. Italy was invaded by the French, and suddenly city defences, advanced cannons and other weapons were all-important, as you can see from Source 6. Each big city recruited engineers and designers to supply it with the latest technology for defence or attack.

The Church

Since the thirteenth century Rome had been the capital of the Catholic Church which was powerful in many parts of Europe. As a result enormous wealth flowed into Rome from all directions. Some of this wealth was used to build grand churches or to decorate them with fine paintings.

The Church was also changing some of its views. For example, in the Middle Ages it had outlawed the dissection of human bodies, but this was now allowed in special cases in certain cities.

The Roman Empire

Although the Roman Empire had fallen apart in the fifth century AD, not all its remains had been destroyed. Roman medical texts, for example, had been copied and improved by Islamic scholars in the Arab world. Trade with the Arab world brought some of these to Italy.

In the Eastern Roman Empire, scholars based in Constantinople had also continued the classical traditions, and from here ideas gradually filtered back to Italy. When Constantinople was captured by the Turks in 1453 many Christian scholars fled to Italy. They brought with them ancient MANUSCRIPTS which dated back to the days of the great Greek and Roman Empires.

Of course, in Italy itself the people were surrounded by many reminders of Roman civilisation.

■ A large number of Roman buildings had survived, even if they were in a partially ruined state (see Source 7). People in Italy became increasingly curious about these.

■ Roman Law was still studied in Italian universities, and formed a basis for the governments of the city states.

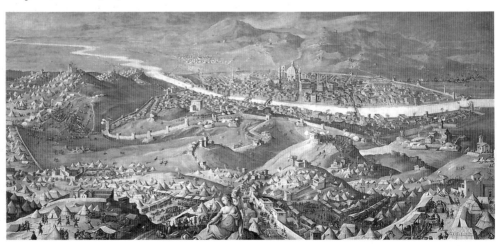

SOURCE 6 The siege of Florence in 1530, painted by Vasari

SOURCE 7 The remains of the PANTHEON in Rome

SOURCE 8 From Vasari's biography of Brunelleschi, who was a successful architect in Italy

66 *When Brunelleschi walked through Rome, seeing for the first time the grandeur of the buildings and the perfect construction of the churches, he kept stopping short in amazement as if thunderstruck . . . and he went without food or sleep and concentrated on the architecture of the past.* 99

1. What does Vasari mean by 'the architecture of the past'?
2. Why do you think Brunelleschi was so impressed by Source 7?

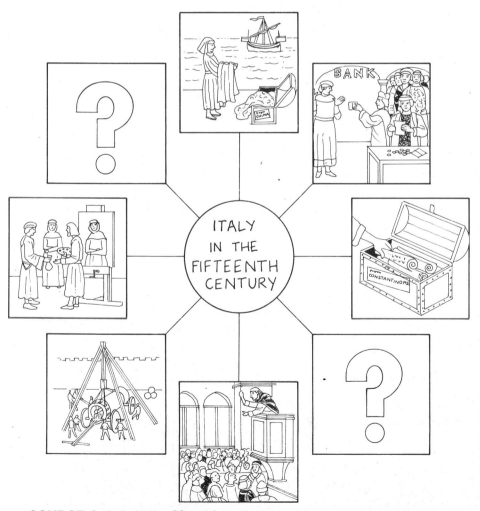

SOURCE 9 Italy in the fifteenth century

Activity

1. Work with a partner. Source 9 summarises some features of fifteenth-century Italy. On your copy of the diagram explain, in your own words, what each picture shows about it.
2. Using the information on the last four pages, in the blank spaces, use a picture and/or words to sum up other features of Italy at this time.
3. Choose one feature in which changes were taking place in the fifteenth century and describe those changes on your diagram.
4. Choose the feature of fifteenth-century Italy which you think might have been the most important in helping Renaissance ideas to develop. Explain your choice.

Leonardo da Vinci: a Renaissance man?

SOURCE 1 One of a set of British postage stamps issued in 1990 showing well-known smiles

Sources 1 and 2 are both by Leonardo da Vinci, one of the best-known figures of the Italian Renaissance. In the next few pages we are going to study Leonardo's life story and to see what it can tell us about the Renaissance. As you read, look out for how the various features of fifteenth-century Italy which you have studied on the previous pages affected his life and work.

Apprenticeship in Florence

Leonardo was born in 1452 near Vinci, a small town in the hills outside Florence. His mother was a peasant woman. His father was a lawyer and a landowner. Leonardo didn't go to school, but from an early age he was a very skilful artist. When he was seventeen his father APPRENTICED him to Andrea del Verrocchio, a well-known painter and sculptor in Florence.

Leonardo was interested in observing people. In his notebook he constantly made sketches of the people and animals he saw in the streets of Florence. With a few strokes of his pen he would try to capture people's smiles or frowns, or the way a body moved. He even sketched the dead body of a hanged criminal.

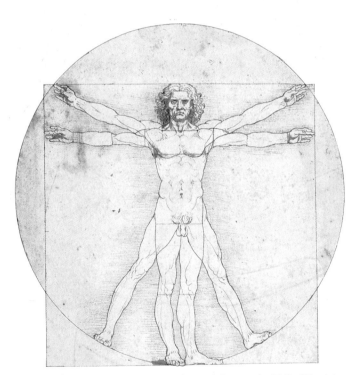

SOURCE 2 From the opening of Granada TV's *World in Action* programme – a programme about modern issues. It shows a 'proportional man' drawn by Leonardo da Vinci

1. Do you recognise Source 1? Do you know which painting it comes from?
2. Why do you think a television company would want to use Source 2 to introduce a programme?

SOURCE 3 The *Baptism of Christ* by Andrea del Verrocchio and his workshop, painted between 1470 and 1476

SOURCE 4 The *Virgin of the Rocks*, painted by Leonardo da Vinci in 1483

It was common for masters to allow the skilled apprentices in their workshop to paint sections of the master's paintings. Art historians think that, as an apprentice, Leonardo painted one of the angels in Verrocchio's picture of the baptism of Christ (Source 3).

Activity

Work in pairs. You are art historians. You know that Leonardo da Vinci painted Source 4. Can you use the clues in Source 4 to work out which of the angels in Source 3 Leonardo probably painted? Look especially at the following:
■ the shape of the angel's head
■ the way the angel's hair is painted
■ the way the angel's clothes are draped.

SOURCE 5 A painting by Botticini. Historians believe that the figure marked with an arrow is Leonardo as a young man. Leonardo was a friend of the artist and it is thought that he posed as a model for the angel

Working in Florence

Most reports say that, as a young man, Leonardo was handsome, blond-haired and blue-eyed. He was fussy about how he looked – he wore bright clothes and hated having paint under his fingernails. He was a skilful horserider and LUTE player.

From the start it was also clear to the people of Florence that Leonardo was a brilliant artist. He was much in demand in Florence. A PATRON is the name given to someone who pays an artist to work for him or her. You can probably work out from the subjects of some of his paintings what kind of patrons Leonardo worked for. For example, he painted a portrait of a rich Florentine woman, Ginevra de' Benci, in 1474, and made several paintings of the Madonna and child (The Virgin Mary and Jesus).

However, Leonardo's interests already ranged beyond painting. He was interested in every aspect of the natural world. He learned about mathematics and science from experiments being done in Florence by the Medici family. For example, they were trying to work out a formula for 'squaring the circle' – drawing a square which was the same area as a given circle. Leonardo carried out his own calculations to do this. He did not succeed, but he remained interested in the problem and it came up again in drawings he made such as Source 2. He also used these experiments to help him design cannons, SIEGE machines and bridges.

LEONARDO DA VINCI: A RENAISSANCE MAN?

From Florence to Milan

In 1482 Leonardo decided to move to Milan, which was one of the richest cities in Italy. Source 6 is from a letter he wrote to the Duke of Milan. Why do you think he wrote this letter?

SOURCE 6 From Leonardo's letter to Lodovico Sforza, Duke of Milan, 1482

66 *Your gracious highness! . . . I shall try to make myself clear to Your Excellency and reveal my secrets.*

1. I have a means of making very light bridges which can be easily moved about.

2. In besieging a place, I know how to cut off the water in the moats . . .

3. I have a means of destroying every tower and fortification.

4. I know of a kind of siege engine which is very light and easy to move and which can be used to hurl fire bombs . . .

5. I know how to construct underground caves and winding passages without making any noise . . .

6. I can make strong, armoured vehicles which cannot be destroyed.

7. I can make large guns for use in battle.

8. I will make stone-throwing machines, catapults, slings and other instruments for you.

9. I know of ships which can be used at sea to attack enemies with great force and strength.

10. In time of peace I believe I can achieve something in architecture.

11. I work as a sculptor in marble, BRONZE and pottery, and can paint as well as other artists you may compare me with.

12. I could also make for you the bronze statue of your father on a horse which you have planned . . . this will make your family even more famous. 99

---

1. From the evidence in Source 6, what did Leonardo think were the Duke of Milan's main needs at this time?
2. Leonardo is mainly remembered today as a great painter. Why then do you think Leonardo only mentions his painting skills briefly, towards the end of the letter?

Leonardo worked in Milan for most of the next sixteen years. He spent twelve years designing and building an enormous dome for Milan Cathedral. In 1496 he painted one of his most famous murals (a wall painting), the *Last Supper*, for the dining room of a convent. At this time, however, Leonardo was experimenting with new types of paint and the mural soon began to flake and fade. You can see what it looks like today in Source 14 on page 19.

He also decorated rooms in the Duke of Milan's palace, and painted portraits of the Duke's friends. He began to make a bronze statue of the Duke's father as he had promised in his letter (Source 6). He made many drawings for it and a full-size clay model. He even had the bronze ready to make the statue. However, before he could make the statue itself the French, who were at war with Milan, attacked the city. The bronze which he had set aside was used to make cannons instead.

Leonardo was also increasingly interested in science. In his 'spare' time – when he did not need to be earning money painting portraits of the rich of Milan, or designing machines for the war with France, or finding ways of strengthening castle walls – he did experiments in mathematics and geometry, and made drawings in his notebooks of fantastic flying machines, finely observed human anatomy, submarines and other war machines (see Source 7). However, many of these were just 'ideas'. They would never have worked. The flying machine, for example, was never built.

---

1. Study the items in Source 7. Give each one a title.
2. Choose two of the items and write a detailed description of each.
3. Draw a timeline from 1450 to 1520, or use the timeline your teacher will give you. Using the information on pages 14–16 mark on Leonardo's birth, then add the following events:
   - he starts his apprenticeship
   - he paints the *Virgin of the Rocks*
   - he paints the *Last Supper*

   Keep your timeline safe so you can add to it.

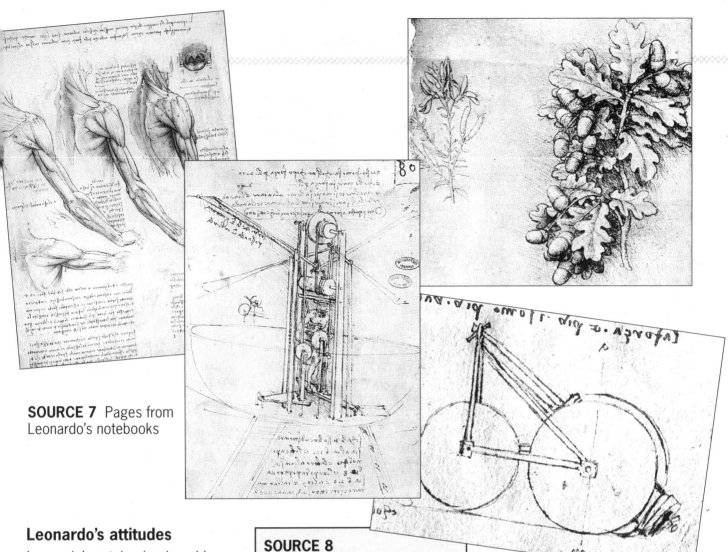

SOURCE 7 Pages from Leonardo's notebooks

Leonardo's attitudes

Leonardo's notebooks show his attitude to the world around him. He approached each new subject with the same attitude – first of all he observed it closely and carefully, and then he recorded what he saw. We take it for granted nowadays that this is a sensible way of finding out about the world, but in the time of the Renaissance it was quite new.

He advised painters to carry notebooks with them wherever they went, just as he did, and to record everything they saw. Leonardo himself filled 3500 pages of notebooks, many of which still survive today. They include drawings such as those in Source 7, and comments such as Sources 8–10.

SOURCE 8

"O painters, when you go into the fields give your attention to the various objects and look carefully in turn first at one thing, and then at another."

SOURCE 9

"A painter who has acquired a knowledge of the nature of the SINEWS, muscles and TENDONS will know exactly which of the sinews are the cause of [any movement of the limbs] and which muscle is the cause of the sinews contracting."

SOURCE 10

"Science is full of error if it has not been born from experience."

SOURCE 11 Leonardo describes a storm which he remembers from when he was four years old

"For ten hours we were attacked by winds. Then the storm brought a sudden flood of water which submerged the lower part of the city. Then came mud, and stones, tangled with roots and branches and fragments of many trees."

1. Using Sources 1–11, make a list of aspects of the natural world in which Leonardo was interested.

LEONARDO DA VINCI: A RENAISSANCE MAN?

Projects in Italy and France

In 1499 Leonardo went to Venice to work for the DOGE (the ruler). The Venetians were afraid they would be invaded by the Turks, and wanted Leonardo to improve their city defences. Leonardo also designed diving suits and submarines so they could attack their enemy's boats below the water, but when they would not try out his ideas he left Venice.

Leonardo had now built a wide reputation. In the next twenty years he worked for rich patrons in Italy and in France on all sorts of projects. Below are some examples.

1500: Florence, redesigned city defences for the Medici family
1502: Milan, military engineer for war against France
1503: Florence, military engineer in war against Pisa; painted the famous portrait of Elizabeth Gioconda which is known as the *Mona Lisa* (see Source 15 on page 19)
1507: France, official painter and engineer for the King of France
1509: Florence, devised a plan for a flying machine
1513: Milan, completed building the Adda Canal
Rome, worked for the brother of the Pope as a painter, and made plans for draining marshes outside the city

Leonardo worked for whoever would pay him. In 1502, for example, he was working for the Duke of Milan helping the city fight against France. In 1506, when the French had captured Milan, he worked for the new French rulers as their chief engineer and painter.

Leonardo also put much energy into his own private interests. He would get up early in the morning – he had designed his own water-powered alarm clock – to make drawings of the human body, study the weather, make mirrors and telescopes to study the stars, design water pumps, or do whatever was his obsession at the time.

He was also very restless. Many of his inventions were never built. He even left most of his paintings unfinished. Either he was too disappointed with the results – they were not perfect enough – or he was attracted away to work on another project.

Leonardo's skills and interests

It is clear from Leonardo's career that he was more than just a painter. Like many other people of the Renaissance he had become so interested in the world around him that he wanted to understand as much about it as he could. He therefore got involved in as many different areas as possible – and applied his skills and interests to a wide range of problems.

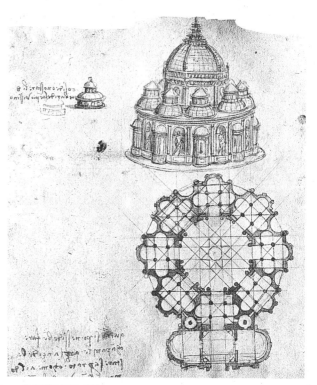

▲SOURCE 12

▼SOURCE 13

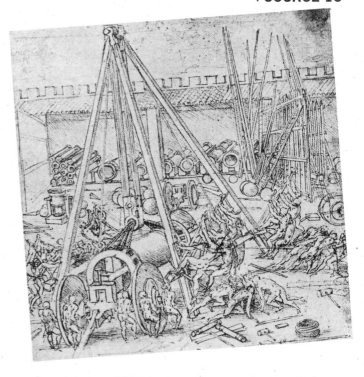

▶ **SOURCE 14**

▼**SOURCE 15**

▶ **SOURCE 16**

SOURCE 17

1. Match each of Sources 12–17 to one of the following captions:
   The *Mona Lisa*.
   Drawings for a sculpture of a horse and rider
   A canal construction machine
   ARTILLERY machines
   A design for a church
   A religious mural called the *Last Supper*

2. Now match each source to one or more of Leonardo's interests:
   military engineering
   civil engineering
   religious art
   portraits
   drawings
   sculpture
   architecture
   anatomy (the study of the human body)

3. Using what you have read about Leonardo, explain how each of the following helped or hindered him:
   a) patronage from rich families
   b) patronage from the Church
   c) war
   d) the time and place in which he was born.

4. Can you think of any other reasons why Leonardo was able to develop his skills and talents so far?

SOURCE 18 Leonardo as an old man. A self-portrait drawn in 1516

Assessments of Leonardo

When studying someone such as Leonardo we have a range of evidence to consider. If you look back at the last eight pages, you will see that we have used many kinds of sources to find out about Leonardo. Each kind was valuable in its own way.

Despite all this evidence, we do not really know very much about Leonardo's personal life. Much of what we know about him comes from a book called *Lives of the Artists* by Giorgio Vasari (1511–74). Vasari lived in Florence and was a painter himself. He tells us, for example, that Leonardo was a vegetarian, that he loved animals and that he was a quiet man. Sources 19–23 are extracts from his biography of Leonardo.

> ### SOURCE 19
>
> ❝ . . . occasionally . . . a single person is given so much beauty, grace and talent that he leaves other men behind. All his actions seem inspired, and indeed everything he does clearly comes from God rather than from human skill. ❞

> ### SOURCE 20
>
> ❝ Leonardo was so lovable that he had everyone's affection. ❞

> ### SOURCE 21
>
> ❝ Clearly it was because of his great knowledge of painting that Leonardo started so many things without finishing them, for he was convinced that his hands, for all their skill, could never perfectly express the clever and wonderful ideas of his imagination. ❞

> ### SOURCE 22
>
> ❝ In appearance he was striking and handsome, and his magnificent presence brought comfort to the most troubled soul . . . He was physically so strong that he could fight back against any violence; with his right hand he would bend the iron ring of a doorbell or a horseshoe as if they were lead. ❞

Leonardo in old age

In 1516 Leonardo went to France, to work for the King, Francis I. Although by now his right hand was paralysed, he continued to write about science. He died on 2 May 1519 at the age of 67.

Leonardo had no children and he was never married – although it is thought he had affairs with both men and women. In his will he ordered 70 masses to be said for his soul all over France and Italy, a treatment usually only given to kings and queens.

1. Mark Leonardo's death on your timeline.
2. Choose five important events from pages 18–20 which show the range of Leonardo's achievements, and add them to your timeline. Explain your choice.

SOURCE 23

Leonardo then painted a Madonna, a very fine work . . . one of the details in this picture was a vase of water containing some flowers, which looked very real. The flowers had on them dewdrops that looked more convincing than the real thing.

Modern historians have looked closely at Leonardo's achievements and have come to different conclusions about him. Read Sources 24 and 25.

SOURCE 24 Speaking on a TV documentary about Leonardo in November 1993, art historian Brian Sewell said about Leonardo

By the age of 30 Leonardo had worked on only two great paintings. Neither of them was finished.

He was a man of dreams and pranks. He was happier inventing toys and japes, and even finishing them, than in ever painting pictures. To a lizard he added silver scales, a horn, and a beard to make it frighteningly monstrous. He took a sheep's intestine and inflated it so hugely that the occupants of a room were pressed into its corners. He made a mechanical lion for the King of France which showered the feet of the King with lilies.

His scheme in 1502 to build canals from the River Arno failed. The river flooded and the scheme was abandoned.

SOURCE 25 The art historian Dr Rosa Maria Letts of the Italian Academy, appearing on the same programme as the speaker of Source 24, said

If you try and compare Leonardo with Michelangelo and Raphael, Leonardo is the greatest artist.

Leonardo was a genius. He was an engineer, a musician, composer, architect, painter and sculptor. He must have been a most fascinating man to meet.

1. Read Sources 19–23. Choose three examples of fact and three of opinion in these sources.
2. How reliable do you think Vasari is as a biographer of Leonardo?
3. Read Sources 24 and 25. Do these historians agree with Vasari?
4. What kind of man do you think Leonardo was? Below are various words. Based on what you have found out about Leonardo from Sources 1–25, choose at least five which you think accurately describe him, then use those words to write your own assessment of his character.
   - observant
   - boring
   - inquisitive
   - shy
   - lucky
   - hard-working
   - artistic
   - quick-tempered
   - inventor
   - linguist
   - amusing
   - impatient
   - greedy
   - mathematician

Activity

It is 1510. Leonardo is applying for a job with the Medici family in Florence. They need someone to:
- paint a portrait of their youngest daughter
- help them design and decorate a grand chapel in Florence
- improve their defences and weapons for war with their rivals in Pisa.

Work in threes to design an application from Leonardo. You should explain how his experience and skills make him ideal for this job. Write a letter and add illustrations if you wish.

Your teacher can give you an application form to fill out if you want it.

How did art change?

LOOK at the two pictures on the cover of this book. They show the same scene (the baptism of Jesus). The one on the left was painted in the Middle Ages. The other was painted about 200 years later during the Renaissance. You can see how the style of painting has changed during the Renaissance. This is just one of the changes that we are going to examine in detail in the next ten pages.

Art in the Middle Ages

In the Middle Ages most art was religious. Artists painted pictures on church walls or as ALTARPIECES at the front of the church. These pictures told a religious story. People who could not read the Bible, or who could not understand the church services (which were usually in Latin) had something to tell them about events described in the Bible, or about the lives of famous saints. The aim of the pictures was a religious one. They were not supposed to be admired for their own sake but for what they taught about God.

In religious art one aim of the artist was to impress people. The artist hoped that if people saw beautiful and expensive religious pictures then they would think that God was great and powerful. This religious purpose affected every aspect of the painting, even, for example, the colours the artist used and the way the painting was arranged.

Gold was the most expensive colour, as real gold was used. Only the best and most costly colour would do for religious pictures, so the artist used as much gold as his patron could afford. The colour valued next was blue, which was made from grinding an expensive stone called lapis lazuli. Medieval artists used this colour for the clothes of important people such as the Virgin Mary.

Even the layout of the picture had a religious purpose. Jesus, the Virgin Mary and saints would be shown bigger than anyone else in the picture. Very important religious figures would also be

► **SOURCE 2** The *Wilton* DIPTYCH. This is one of the most highly valued medieval paintings today. The National Gallery in London has recently spent much time and money cleaning and restoring it

St. Edmund

St. Edward

John the Baptist (Richard's patron saint)

Richard II

the royal saints of England

▶ SOURCE 1 Even paintings which showed SECULAR (non-religious) subjects often had a religious purpose. Although this painting shows an everyday scene, it was in fact painted to decorate a medieval prayer book. Why might such a book be decorated?

the flag of St. George of England

Mary, the mother of Jesus

angels

Jesus

given a halo around their heads, or might be shown holding symbolic objects.

Less important people, on the other hand, might look identical to one another – because their features, or how they were feeling, did not matter to the artist.

In the same way background was not important to the religious artist. It would only have distracted people's attention from the characters in the picture, so it was kept very simple.

As a result, to modern eyes medieval pictures might look flat and unreal. In the Middle Ages people would not have thought this way; looking at the medieval picture of the baptism of Christ (on the cover) a viewer would have been interested in the story the artist was telling – not in whether it looked real.

1. Study Source 2 carefully. Using the information in the paragraphs above, write a detailed description of the picture. Explain why you think the artist has used particular colours, arranged his characters and painted his background in the way he has.

HOW DID ART CHANGE?

Art in the Renaissance

In the fourteenth century, first in Italy and then in other parts of Europe, art began to change. One reason for this was that the Italian artists began to look back to the way in which classical Greek and Roman artists had worked. Not many classical paintings had survived, but there were descriptions from which artists tried to copy them.

In the Renaissance the subjects of paintings became more varied. Renaissance artists still painted religious pictures but they also depicted the ancient stories of Roman and Greek gods and heroes. What do you think is happening in Source 3?

Even more importantly, they were adopting the attitude of the classical artists. Roman and Greek artists had been interested in people and in the natural world. Renaissance artists were too. Classical artists had tried to show what people looked like, how they moved their bodies, or how their facial expressions changed. Renaissance artists did too.

Like the classical artists, Renaissance artists wanted their pictures to look realistic. In the Middle Ages the artists had devoted most of their energy to making the people who looked at their pictures think about God. Now the artists were putting their effort into making characters, objects, animals, even backgrounds look like they did in real life.

SOURCE 3 *Apollo and Daphne* by Antonio del Pollaiuolo (1432–98)

They found their own ways of doing this. Leonardo da Vinci, for example, made detailed drawings of muscles and SINEWS, of stormy skies, of mountains in early-morning sunlight, or of how trees or water moved in the wind. A medieval artist would never have thought it worth spending time on such activities.

Renaissance artists also developed a new set of rules for making their pictures look more real. This was known as PERSPECTIVE (see Source 4). Using perspective artists could give their pictures depth and distance. Although classical artists may have known about perspective, no record of that knowledge survived, so the Renaissance artists had to develop these rules on their own.

▶ **SOURCE 4** The *Annunciation with St Emidius*, painted by Carlo Crivelli in about 1486. It was an altarpiece commissioned by a church in Ascoli, a town in central Italy

Parallel lines appear to meet in the far distance, as they do if you look down a road or a railway track

Figures and objects in the distance appear smaller than those in the foreground, just as they do in real life. Notice how the artist shows off his new skill by drawing pairs of objects to compare such as the window bars or the birds

1. What is happening in Source 4?
2. What do you think the artist's purpose was in painting this picture?
3. How might this have been different from the intentions of a medieval artist?
4. From the evidence on these two pages, where did Renaissance artists get their ideas from?

SOURCE 5 The *Nativity of Christ* from the Winchester Bible

SOURCE 6 The *Madonna of the Meadow*, painted in Italy by Giovanni Bellini

SOURCE 7 The *Virgin and Child*, painted in Italy by Masaccio

Activity

None of the changes we have described took place overnight. They happened over centuries. And they happened more quickly in Italy than they did in other countries of Europe.

Sources 5–7 all show the same subject – the Virgin Mary, and Jesus as a baby. One of the pictures comes from the Middle Ages, one from the early Renaissance period and one from the late Renaissance. Can you work out which is which?

Work in threes. Take one picture each.

1. Write notes about your picture under the following headings:
   - what the baby looks like
   - colours used
   - background
   - use of perspective.

   Your teacher can give you an outline sheet to help you if you wish.

2. Put the pictures in chronological order and use your notes above to explain your order.

3. Write a paragraph explaining how art changed during the Renaissance, using the information on pages 22–25 and Sources 5–7 as examples.

How did a Renaissance artist work?

ONE of the most famous works of the Italian Renaissance is the vast painting on the ceiling of the Sistine Chapel in Rome. It was painted – almost single-handedly – by Michelangelo. It took him four years.

Source 1 describes how he did it. It comes from a novel called *The Agony and the Ecstasy* by Irving Stone. In order to write his novel the author spent a number of years thoroughly researching Michelangelo's life and work. The most important evidence he used in writing it were 485 letters written by Michelangelo himself.

Before he painted the Sistine Chapel, Michelangelo had been most famous as a sculptor. At the start of this extract he has been called to Pope Julius' palace to be given his instructions.

SOURCE 1 Edited extracts from *The Agony and the Ecstasy* by Irving Stone, a novel written in 1961

❝ **1508**

'You will paint the twelve apostles on the ceiling of the Sistine Chapel, and decorate it with the usual designs. We will pay you three thousand large gold ducats.'

'I am a sculptor, not a painter.'

'You dare to question my judgement?' The Pope glared at Michelangelo.

'You must help me draw up a list of assistants,' Michelangelo said to his friend Granacci. 'And here is a list of colours to send for. These colours sent to us by the suppliers in Rome are no good at all.'

'It's not easy to find five painters free at the same time,' Granacci told him. 'I'll have to go to Florence. It may take a couple of months, but I promise to bring back everyone you want.'

Summer pressed down on Rome. Half the city became ill with clogged heads and pains in the chest. Michelangelo climbed the ladder to his platform at dawn. He spent the airless days making scale models of the ceiling. At night he worked in the back garden of his house, making designs for six thousand square feet of ceiling that had to be replastered and made pretty.

In September Granacci returned with a full team in tow, and the team set to work. Michelangelo laid out on the table before them the scale drawings of the ceiling. To each of his assistants he gave part of the VAULT for decoration. He felt certain he could cover the ceiling in seven months. Then he could go back to sculpture.

The group worked well together. Michi mixed the plaster on the scaffold after hauling the sacks up the ladder. Rosselli expertly laid the plaster each day. He watched it dry and kept it moist if necessary. Even Jacopo worked hard to copy the colours into the outline drawings.

1509

[The team completed a large section of the ceiling. Although Michelangelo had done what the Pope had asked for, he was not very pleased with it. He needed to rethink his entire plan. He went walking in the hills near Rome.]

The further Michelangelo walked, the clearer his problem became to him. His helpers would have to go. Donnino was fine as a draughtsman but he lacked courage in colour. Jacopo did no more work at thirty-five than he had at fifteen. Tedesco painted poorly. Sangallo dared to do anything but he was still inexperienced. Bugiardini was reliable but he could only paint flat walls and windows. Michelangelo had to work alone.

He walked, higher and higher into the mountains. As he stood on the peak the sun came up and the countryside came to life in pale pinks and tawny browns. 'What an artist God was when he created the universe,' he thought. And Michelangelo knew that there was a theme to conquer that vault – to overwhelm its ugliness and put in its place the glory of God creating the Sun, the moon, the Earth, and the evolving of man and of woman.

Michelangelo told Granacci that the team was finished. Granacci was staggered. 'Working alone it will take you forty years.'

'No. Closer to four.'

Now Michelangelo returned to the Sistine to look at the vault with sharper eyes. He had to transform it with the only material available to him. Paint.

Ideas now came rushing to him all at once, so tumultuously that he could hardly move his hands fast enough to set them down.

He began with the story of the Flood. By March he had the drawings enlarged and ready to be transferred to the ceiling. Michi ground colours below. Michelangelo was on his platform, sixty feet above the floor. He began at the point of the picture that interested him most: the trunk of a storm-twisted tree extending towards Noah's Ark, a young man climbing the tree in a desperate effort to get to the highest point.

At the end of the first week a biting north wind arose. In the morning he walked to the Sistine, not sure whether he could get his hands warm enough to hold a brush. But when he reached the top of the platform he saw that his panel was ruined. His plaster and paints were not drying. Instead there was a moist dripping at the edges of his stormy tree.

The Flood took Michelangelo thirty-two days of consecutive painting. Pope Julius had been eagerly waiting to see the first fresco. He climbed the ladder to the scaffolding. He studied the figures.
'Will the rest of the ceiling be as good?'
'Better. I am still learning about proper perspective at this height.'
'I am pleased with you, my son.'

1510
Michelangelo returned to his scaffold, determined that nothing should divert him. For thirty days he painted from light to darkness. He painted squatting down, his thighs tight against his belly, his eyes a few inches from the ceiling. Then he lay flat on his back, his knees in the air to steady his painting arm. He no longer bothered to shave, so his beard caught a constant drip of paint and water. No matter which way he leaned, crouched, lay or knelt on his feet, knees or back, his body was always under strain. For thirty days he slept in his clothes, without even taking off his boots. When he'd finished the section Michi pulled his boots off for him and the skin came with them.

Then he thought he was going blind. A letter arrived and he could not read it. He threw himself on the bed. What was he doing to himself? He had refused to paint the simple commission of the Pope and now he would come out of this chapel a gnarled, twisted, ugly, blind dwarf, deformed and aged by his own stupidity.

1511
Julius was reported to be dying of malaria. Michelangelo became anxious. If Pope Julius died, what would happen to his payment? He had only an oral agreement with the Pope, not a written contract.

It was a race against death. During the warm, light days of May and June he spent seventeen consecutive hours on the scaffold, taking food and a chamber pot up with him so that he would not have to descend. He painted like a man possessed.

1512
During the grey Winter months of 1512 the Pope, strong again, kept insisting that Michelangelo complete his ceiling quickly, quickly! Then one day Julius climbed the ladder unannounced.
'When will you finish? You have already taken four years. It is my will that you finish it in seven days.'
'It will be done when it will be done.'
'Do you want to be thrown down from this scaffolding? On All Saints' Day I shall celebrate Mass here,' declared the Pope.

Michelangelo ordered Michi to take down the scaffolding. The next day Julius stopped by.
'Don't some of the decorations need to be brightened with gold?'
'Holy Father, in those times men did not bedeck themselves with gold.'
'It will look poor.'
'Those whom I have painted were poor,' said Michelangelo. 'They were holy men.'

On All Saints' Day official Rome dressed itself in its finest robes for the dedication of the Sistine Chapel. Michelangelo rose early, went to the baths, shaved off his beard, donned his blue clothes. But he did not go to the Sistine. Instead he walked out under the balcony of his house, pulled back the tarpaulin covering the marble he had waited years to carve. He took up his hammer and chisel . . .
99

Activity

1. A film is going to be made of this novel. In pairs prepare a story-board for this section of the story. Use 6–8 frames.
2. Use your story-board to write a paragraph or two about how a Renaissance artist worked, including the following:
   - the patron commissioning the work
   - planning the work
   - preparing the walls and paints
   - completing the painting.

Renaissance portrait gallery

In the Middle Ages artists very seldom painted portraits. When they did – even when painting pictures of important people – they would not try to paint a likeness of the named person. They might not even have seen the person of whom they were painting a picture. In paintings which included a number of figures, Source 2 on page 23, for example, the faces of the people look almost exactly the same.

Renaissance artists, on the other hand, developed a great interest in painting portraits. They were keen observers, and they wanted their portraits to be true likenesses of the people they were painting. They also wanted to give portraits some character and life.

> **SOURCE 1** From Vasari's biography of Leonardo da Vinci
>
> ❝As soon as Leonardo was prepared to paint any figure, he set out for places where he knew that people of that sort gathered together and carefully examined their faces, their manners, their movement. He noted everything in pencil in the little book which he carried at all times.❞

> **SOURCE 2** Adapted from the notebooks of Leonardo da Vinci
>
> ❝A good painter has two main objects to paint: the person, **and** the way the person is feeling.
> The first is easy.
> The second is hard because the painter has to represent feelings by the position of the body and the movement of face and limbs.❞

What the Renaissance artists tried to do was to paint people with expressions on their faces and with their own individual character. As the artists' interest in portrait painting increased, so their skills and techniques improved. The artist would get the subject to 'POSE' for his or her portrait, observe the subject closely, and make lots of drawings in preparation for the final painting.

Artists – first of all those in Northern Europe – developed new oil-based paints, which were more suitable for painting hair, skin or clothing. They used layers of paint so that the colour from the earlier layers glowed through the top one, giving depth and texture to the portrait. Leonardo da Vinci used a new shading technique called SFUMATO which allowed him to paint areas of light and shade effectively (see Source 4 on page 15 for example).

It became fashionable for rich people to have their portraits painted as a way of showing off their wealth. A family would have a portrait painted to commemorate a special occasion such as a wedding – much as we might make a wedding video or compile a photo album today. Carnations in a picture were often a sign that someone was about to be married. Sometimes wealthy people who gave a religious picture to a church even asked to have themselves included somewhere in the painting.

Sources 3–6 are portraits painted by Renaissance artists. All but one are Italian.

1. Choose Source 3 or Source 6 and explain how it is different from a medieval painting such as Source 2 on page 23.
2. Which of Sources 3–6 do you think is the earliest? Explain your choice.
3. Consider how a person might dress to have his or her portrait painted. Judging by the clothes people are wearing in these portraits, which of them do you think is the most wealthy? Explain your choice.
4. Look at the portrait of Georg Gisze (Source 3). Study the objects in the picture carefully – they relate to his work. What do you think his job was?
5. After reading the information about Renaissance portraits, why do you think Georg Gisze had his portrait painted?
6. As you can see from your answers to questions 3–5, portraits can tell us what a person looked like, but they can tell us other things as well. What other historical information do the portraits in Sources 3–6 give us?

▲**SOURCE 3** *Georg Gisze* by Hans Holbein the Younger

▲**SOURCE 4** *Portrait of a young woman* by Antonio del Pollaiuolo

▼**SOURCE 6** *Portrait of a lady* by Titian

▼**SOURCE 5** *The Doge Leonardo Loredan* by Giovanni Bellini

A tour through Florence: how did architecture change?

DURING the Renaissance the people of Italy felt they were rediscovering their country's history. Proud of what the ancient Romans had achieved, they made great efforts to find out about and copy as many aspects of Roman life as they could.

For Renaissance architects this was made easier by the fact that they were surrounded by ancient Roman buildings, although some of these were better preserved than others. For centuries architects visited Rome to look at and measure buildings like the COLOSSEUM and the PANTHEON (see Source 7 on page 13).

Architects used these classical models to develop a Renaissance style of architecture. They followed Roman ideas about:

■ symmetry – one side is a mirror image of the other
■ the shapes of buildings
■ the details and decoration on buildings.

They also liked to show their great engineering skills by copying impressive features of Roman buildings such as domes and arches.

SOURCE 1 The Roman forum in the first half of the sixteenth century, drawn by Netherlands artist Marten van Heemskerck

a) Classical columns

There were three styles (or 'orders') of column, known as DORIC, IONIC and CORINTHIAN depending on how the top of the column was decorated

pediment

capital

column

DORIC   IONIC   CORINTHIAN

b) A symmetrical Roman building with a dome

c) A set of Roman arches

SOURCE 2 The main features of classical architecture

In the Middle Ages the most important buildings had been

■ churches and cathedrals which had pointed arches, elaborate decoration, and towers and spires which seemed to be trying to reach heaven
■ castles which were built solidly with battlements and towers for defence.

In order to investigate how the Renaissance changed architecture we are going to be guided around Florence by an English visitor, Thomas Hoby.

Thomas Hoby was only aged seventeen when he set off in 1547 on a six-year tour of Europe. At this time it was fashionable for the young sons of rich families to complete their education by visiting Europe. Through most of his travels Thomas wrote a diary. In 1548 he wrote, 'After I had stayed a year in Padua and Venice and had [gained] some understanding of the Italian tongue I thought it wise to visit the renowned country of Tuscany'.

He travelled by boat down the coast from Venice to Ferrara. Then he transferred to a covered horse-drawn wagon for the journey inland. The journey was slow and uncomfortable. Thomas was crammed together with the other passengers on hard benches.

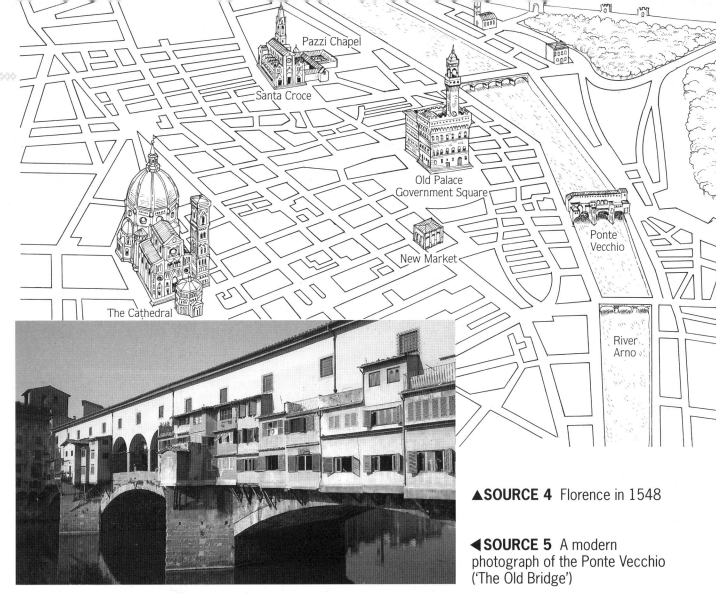

▲SOURCE 4 Florence in 1548

◄SOURCE 5 A modern photograph of the Ponte Vecchio ('The Old Bridge')

En route the travellers stopped in Bologna, where Thomas visited the university, which had some of the most advanced scholars in Europe. Then they travelled on into Tuscany, passing castles built by the Medici family. Finally in the distance Thomas saw the walls and the buildings of Florence.

> **SOURCE 3** From Thomas Hoby's diary, 1549
>
> 66 *The fair city of Florence is built on the River Arno. Three bridges cross the river in different places. The city is surrounded to the east and the north by pleasant hills covered with fruit trees . . .* 99

1. Source 2 on page 10 shows you the kind of view Thomas Hoby would have got of Florence as he approached it. Source 3 is the beginning of his description of the city. Write down five more things that Source 2 on page 10 would tell him about Florence.

Thomas stayed five or six days in Florence, lodging with another Englishman, and exploring much of the city. The rest of this account is an imaginative reconstruction of what Thomas might have done in a day of walking around Florence.

You can find the places he visits on the map in Source 4.

To get to the heart of the city Thomas crosses the River Arno. He visits the shops on the bridge (Source 5). The shopkeeper tells him that once the shops were all butchers' shops, but that the goldsmiths are beginning to take them over. This bridge is called the 'Old Bridge' because it was the first bridge to be built across the River Arno in 1345. You can see from Source 3 how impressed Thomas was that Florence now had three bridges.

2. How do you think people crossed the Arno before 1345?

SOURCE 6 Government Square in Florence, painted in the sixteenth century

Thomas makes his way to the heart of the city, Government Square (Piazza della Signoria). The government of Florence meets in the Old Palace (centre right in Source 6).

The picture shows a public execution taking place in the square. This was a very unusual event. Thomas did not see such an execution. When he saw the square it would have been crowded with street traders and workers. Just off Government Square he sees the brand new market building (Source 7). In it the traders are selling silk and gold.

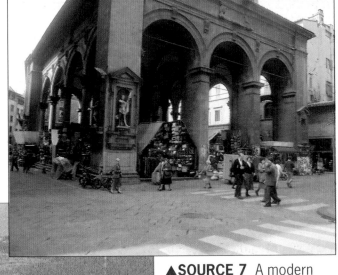

▲**SOURCE 7** A modern photograph of the New Market

1. Look at Source 6. What does the Old Palace remind you of?
2. When, roughly, do you think it was built?
3. Look at Source 7. It is a Renaissance building. How is it different from the Old Palace?

SOURCE 8 The Cathedral

Thomas now makes his way up one of the city's main streets towards the great glory of Florence, the Cathedral (the Duomo; Source 8). It is also known as the Church of Santa Maria del Fiore. With its enormous dome it totally dominates the city.

Most of the cathedral was built in stages between 1375 and 1421. It was then complete except for the dome (or cupola). However, the cathedral was so wide that many architects did not think it would be possible to build a dome across it. They thought it would collapse in the middle.

Filippo Brunelleschi, a clever Florentine architect, solved the problem using ideas he had learned from studying the way the ancient Romans built domes. He constructed scaffolding which helped to get the huge pieces of stone to the top of the tower. Inside he built winding stairs which you can still climb today.

The dome was completed in 1436. Many architects followed Brunelleschi's example, and soon domed buildings were appearing all over Europe. You can probably think of some in Britain.

> **SOURCE 9** From Thomas Hoby's diary, using his original spelling
>
> 66 *Within Florence is the faire church called Santa Maria del Fiore, all of Marble. In the toppe of yt is the marvellous peece of worke called the Cupola, worthie to be seen by all travellars. Outside this church there is a rounde temple dedicated to Saint John the Baptist.* 99

From the cathedral Thomas makes his way back towards the river, past the Church of Santa Croce and the Pazzi Chapel. He walks through the side streets and little squares of Florence. There are barbers and dressmakers; and butchers displaying their meat on tables in front of their shops. Thomas wants something to eat, so he calls in at one of the many small inns for a meal of cold meats, bread and wine. In his diary he praises the local wine, Torbiano, as 'one of the most pleasant and delicate in Italy'.

Activity
Design a postcard from Thomas Hoby. One side will have one or more pictures of Florence on it. On the other side Thomas writes to a friend, describing what impresses him most about the city.

What effect has Renaissance architecture had on later building?

SOURCE 10 The White House, Washington DC – the official residence of the President of the USA. It was built in the nineteenth century

SOURCE 11 A house on a modern estate, built in the 1980s

1. Compare Sources 10 and 11 with the Renaissance buildings in Florence such as Source 7. What Renaissance features have been copied in these modern buildings?
2. What impression do you think the people who built the buildings shown in Sources 10 and 11 were trying to create by using these classical features?

What was the role of women during the Renaissance?

WHEN people talk about the changes which the Renaissance brought, they are often referring to the new developments in art and architecture that we have been studying in the last 14 pages. Indeed, it is easy to see how these things were affected by the Renaissance.

Now we are going to approach the Renaissance and its changes from a different angle. What was life like for ordinary people during this period? Sources 1–12 concern the lives and experiences of some Italian women in the fourteenth to sixteenth centuries. What can these sources tell you?

Women as slaves

There were many slaves in Italy, both men and women. Slaves could be bought cheaply in the markets at Venice or Genoa, where the trade was mainly in girls and young women. They came from Greece, Turkey, Russia or Central Asia.

In legal documents which listed people's possessions, slaves were put in the same category as domestic animals. Legally a slave owner could 'own, sell, exchange, dispose of, judge' his slaves, 'and do with them whatsoever may please him and his heirs'.

Many slave girls became pregnant by their masters. Cosimo de' Medici, who became ruler of Florence in 1434, lived in Rome, away from his family, for two years. There he was looked after by a slave girl called Maddalena, who had been bought for him in Venice. She bore him a son, Carlo, who was brought up and educated with his other children.

A slave girl living with a wealthy family would often be better off (for example, be better fed and healthier) than many poor women living in Italy who were not slaves.

> **SOURCE 2** Advice on the treatment of slave girls by Fra Bernadino, a travelling preacher from Siena
>
> *Is there sweeping to be done? Then make your slave sweep. Are there pots to be scoured? Then make her scour them. Are there vegetables to be cleaned or fruit to be peeled? Then set her to them. Laundry? Hand it to her. Make her look after the children and everything else.*
>
> *If you don't get her used to the work, she will become a lazy little lump of flesh. Don't give her any time off, I tell you. As long as you keep her on the go, she won't waste her time leaning out of the window.*

> **SOURCE 3** From the papers of Francesco di Marco Datini, a fourteenth-century merchant from Prato, near Florence
>
> *The slave you sent is sick, or rather covered in boils, so that we can find none who would have her. We will sell or barter her as best we can, and send you the account. Furthermore, I hear she is with child, two months gone or more, and therefore she will not be worth selling.*

SOURCE 1 Women slaves at work – details from paintings of the Renaissance period

1. What sort of work do Sources 1 and 2 suggest female slaves were expected to do?
2. What do Sources 1–3 tell us about the attitudes of some owners to female slaves?
3. We have more evidence about the lives of slave girls than about the lives of poor women who were not slaves in Renaissance Italy. Why do you think this is?

Renaissance marriage

In rich families a daughter's marriage was arranged for her by her parents. The better off the family, the less choice a girl would have in choosing her husband. Powerful families would use their daughter's marriage to strengthen a political alliance or to make trading links.

Daughters had to be provided with DOWRIES to attract a suitable husband. Families could not always afford dowries for all their daughters, and it was quite usual for younger daughters to become nuns because their parents could not afford for them to marry.

Not many girls received an education. Unmarried girls from rich families were rarely seen in public at all except on their way to MASS, and then they wore veils to hide their faces. In some households even Mass was said at home and the young daughters' only exercise was walking in the garden of their homes. Girls were considered ready for marriage at the age of twelve, although it was more usual for them to marry when they were fifteen or sixteen.

When they got married, all girls – even if they were quite poor – would be presented with a *cassone*, a carved wooden wedding chest to be filled with clothes, linen or crockery. For a poor girl this would be a simple chest. For a wealthy girl it would be beautifully decorated.

---

1. According to the information and sources above:
   a) How did men choose their wives in Renaissance Italy?
   b) What were the advantages and disadvantages of being a married woman?
2. Source 6 was written in 1974. Do you think an historian writing today would write in the same way? Explain your answer.

SOURCE 4 A wedding chest showing a marriage taking place in Florence. Can you see the wedding couple, the servants preparing food and the musicians? Notice the fashionable clothes of the couple, who clearly come from wealthy families

---

SOURCE 5 A modern historian describes the reasons Lorenzo de' Medici married Clarice Orsini, the daughter of a powerful family from Rome

" Not only would he avoid arousing any jealousy in Florence where there would be other marriageable daughters whom he had rejected, but he would be forming an alliance with a family of great influence. The Orsini had huge estates. They could raise soldiers as well as money and in Clarice's uncle, Cardinal Latino, they would have an influence among the Pope's advisers.

Lorenzo would naturally have preferred a better-looking and more intellectual bride, but having caught sight of her one day at Mass, he agreed that she was acceptable. Once a dowry of 6000 florins was settled, he married her by proxy in Rome. [Proxy means someone stood in for him at the wedding ceremony. He was not there himself.] "

SOURCE 6 Written by E.R. Chamberlin in *Florence in the time of the Medici*, published in 1974

" In all families, at all times, it is the woman who runs the home. A Florentine woman was fortunate in that she was accepted on almost equal terms with men. She had no say in running the city, her property became her husband's (for he was her legal master) and no decent woman would go to places of public entertainment. But in her home she entertained her husband's guests and was accepted into their conversation. "

Sources 7–9 are extracts from letters between Margherita Datini and her husband. We can find out from these how far this marriage followed the general pattern outlined on the previous pages.

Margherita was the wife of Francesco di Marco Datini, a merchant from Prato, near Florence. She was 25 years younger than her husband.

Francesco lived in Florence because of his business – trading in armour, luxury goods, spices, linen and pictures. Many letters passed between him and his wife concerning the running of the house in Prato.

Margherita herself was unable to have any children, although her husband's illegitimate daughter, Ginevra, and the daughter of a friend, Caterina, were brought up in their household. She had three or four servants and several slaves to help her run the house. It was a household made up mainly of women.

> **SOURCE 7** From Francesco to Margherita
>
> *Tomorrow morning send back the small jar of dried raisins and the bread. And send the barrel of vinegar, . . . remember to wash the mules' feet with hot water . . . have my HOSE made and soled. Give some MILLET to the nag and see it is well washed . . .*

> **SOURCE 8** From Francesco to Margherita
>
> *Remember to go to bed at a sensible time and rise early and don't let the door be opened until you are up and about. And look after everything; don't let them [the slaves] mess about. You know what Bartolomea is; she will say she is going to one place and then go elsewhere . . . Now conduct yourself in such a way that I need not scold.*

> **SOURCE 9** From Margherita to Francesco
>
> *You write to me that Guido's wife has never caused him any trouble. I believe he is speaking the truth; but I think that he has caused less grief to her, than she to him. For Guido knows how to rule a wife. He keeps his wife as a woman, and not as an innkeeper's wife! For it is fifteen years since I first came here, and I have always lived here as if in an inn.*

1. List ways in which this marriage is similar to or different from the description in Source 6. Can you give reasons for any differences?

Women patrons and artists

There were many women who were PATRONS. Isabella d'Este was probably the most famous. She was married to the Duke of Mantua and when he was away – often for long periods – she helped govern the state of Mantua. She had received a broad education, and was very interested in the new ideas of the Renaissance. She paid for work by many different painters, including Leonardo da Vinci.

During the Renaissance a number of women also became successful artists. There is documentary evidence of 23 female sculptors and painters working in Bologna in the sixteenth and seventeenth centuries. These included Lavinia Fontana, who became an official painter to the Pope. Bologna was however an exceptional town, which had a progressive attitude towards women. Its university had accepted female students as early as the thirteenth century.

Vasari's *Lives of the Artists* – biographies of all those whom he considered to be important figures of Renaissance art – included a number of female artists. One of them was Sofonisba Anguissola.

Anguissola's father was a nobleman in Cremona in northern Italy. Her parents encouraged her and her five sisters to become painters. This was probably because they were unable to raise the big dowries needed for good marriages.

At the age of thirteen Sofonisba was APPRENTICED to a local portrait painter for three years. She in turn helped train her sisters to paint. Two of them, Lucia and Europa, also became renowned artists.

Sofonisba attracted much attention as an artist. She sent copies of her drawings to Michelangelo himself for his criticism. She seems to have made many self-portraits – and she sent one of them to Pope Julius III in 1555.

▶ **SOURCE 10** A portrait painted by Sofonisba Anguissola. It shows her sister, dressed as a nun

In 1559 she was invited to the court of Philip of Spain at Madrid. He was impressed by her portrait-painting and gave her a large allowance from the royal treasury and an enormous diamond.

In 1570 she married a Sicilian nobleman with a dowry provided by the King of Spain. He died only four years later. She remarried; her second husband was the captain of a ship.

The King of Spain wanted her to return to his court, but she preferred to stay in Genoa. There she carried on her work as a painter, until she gradually became blind in later life.

SOURCE 11 From the *Guardian* newspaper, 1992

66 *The famous Dutch artist Anthony van Dyck was a frequent guest who greatly admired Sofonisba's work, stating that he learned more about the principles of art from talking to her than he had from any of his teachers.* 99

SOURCE 12 From the biography of Sofonisba Anguissola in Vasari's *Lives of the Artists*, 1568

66 *Not only does she design and paint from the life, and copy the works of others with the most consummate skill and the most perfect success, but she has herself composed and executed most admirable works of her own invention in painting.* 99

1. Compare Sources 11 and 12. Do van Dyck and Vasari agree or disagree about Anguissola?
2. When Vasari's book was translated into English, only a selection of biographies was included. Sofonisba – and all the other women artists in the original book – were left out. Which of the following do you think is the most likely reason why the translators left out Sofonisba:
a) because she was a woman
b) because she was not a very good artist
c) because they did not have enough space to include every artist
d) because people's artistic tastes had changed?

Activity
You have now studied the lives of several women who lived in Italy during the Renaissance.

Working in groups, compare the lives of the following three women:

Maddalena – the slave and mistress of Cosimo de' Medici

Margherita Datini – the wife of the merchant of Prato

Sofonisba Anguissola – artist.

Divide a sheet of paper in three, and make notes about the lives of the three women, for example on their social status, their childhood and marriage, their education, their work.

Is there any evidence that these women's lives were affected by the changes of the Renaissance?

Did health and medicine improve?

The plague

In the Renaissance period life was generally much shorter than today. Many people did not live beyond the age of 30. In difficult times something like half of all babies born died before they reached the age of one. War, starvation and disease were all major causes of death in fourteenth-century Italy. One of the most feared diseases of all was the plague, which struck Italian cities regularly from the middle of the fourteenth century when the Black Death was rife all over Europe.

Nowadays historians believe that the Black Death probably included two different diseases. One was carried by fleas which lived on rats. The other was caught by breathing germs sneezed out by an infected person. However, people in early Renaissance Italy had many of their own explanations for the plague and how to avoid catching it, as you can see from Sources 1 and 2.

Source 1 was written by one of the most famous writers of the early Renaissance period – Boccaccio. He was in Florence when the first outbreak of plague swept through the city in 1348. His father, stepmother and uncle all died.

A few years later he wrote the DECAMERON – a story about a group of young men and women who move out of Florence into the countryside to avoid the plague. Source 1 is from his introduction to the *Decameron*. The three extracts show some of the effects of the Black Death in Florence and how people tried to deal with it.

---

1. Use Sources 1 and 2 to make a list of what people in the fourteenth century thought were:
   a) the causes of the plague
   b) cures for the plague.

SOURCE 1 Adapted from Boccaccio's introduction to the *Decameron*

66■ *In 1348 in the worthy city of Florence, the most noble in all Italy, there arrived the most deadly plague. Either because of the movements of the planets, or because our sinful deeds had made God so angry he decided to punish us. The plague had started some years earlier in the East. It took many lives there. Then it spread relentlessly from place to place towards the West.*

■ *No clever or man-made measures could work against this plague, although rubbish was cleared from the city by specially appointed officials, sick people were stopped from entering the city, and much advice was circulated to safeguard health. Neither did humble prayers to God or processions have any effect, for in the early spring of 1348 the plague's terrible effects began to reveal themselves in a ghastly and incredible manner. Neither doctors' advice nor the power of medicine had any effect.*

■ *What made this plague spread even more quickly was that the sick only had to be in the company of the healthy for the latter to be infected – just as fire consumes dry material when it is nearby. Merely touching the clothes or any other thing which had been touched by those with the disease seemed to infect one with it.* 99

SOURCE 2 A procession of 'flagellants'. These people believed that the plague was a punishment sent by God. They whipped each other as a way of asking God to forgive them

This was the first outbreak of plague in the cities of Italy. It was to return at regular intervals throughout the Renaissance period.

Fifty years later the Florentine merchant Francesco Datini had seen six outbreaks of the Black Death, or *Moria* as it was called in Italy. Then in 1399 there was yet another outbreak in Florence. Datini was in his 60s. His letters to and from his friends have survived to this day (see Source 3). Do they show evidence that there was a greater understanding of the plague as a result of the six previous outbreaks?

The Datini family was urged by friends to leave Florence. Francesco's wife Margherita was in favour of staying. She believed that they would have more help for their bodies and souls in Florence than elsewhere – presumably because there were doctors in Florence to treat the body and priests to look after the soul.

Francesco, however, decided to go on a PILGRIMAGE to a holy shrine. He dressed entirely in white linen, and walked all the way barefoot. Many others in Florence did the same. They believed that the pilgrimage would please God and he would take away the plague.

In June 1400 – with the plague still raging – Francesco revised his will, leaving all his wealth to charity. He then took his wife and his whole household to Bologna, a city which was free from plague. They survived.

Other families were not so lucky, as the letter in Source 3 shows, written to Francesco by a friend who stayed in Florence.

About 11,000 people (out of a population of 60–100,000) had died in Florence by 1401. The leaders of the city ordered new doors to be built for their cathedral as a plea to God not to let the plague return.

---

1. What was the attitude to the plague of:
   ■ Francesco Datini
   ■ Ser Lappo Mazzei
   ■ Mazzei's eldest son
   ■ the leaders of Florence?
2. Is there any evidence that, between 1348 and 1400, ideas had changed about:
   ■ the causes of the plague; and
   ■ cures for the plague?

Doctors and hospitals

In 1400 Florence had 60 registered doctors of medicine. This may not seem many for a population of 60,000 people, but in the fifteenth century few people would consult a doctor if they were ill. The poor of course could not afford their fees. But, as we have already seen, most people – rich and poor alike – believed that terrible events like the plague were caused by factors such as God being angry with them, or the movements of the planets. St Bernard, a Christian writer, said in the twelfth century, 'To buy drugs or to consult with doctors doesn't fit with religion'. The best people to explain what was going wrong would not be the doctors but the religious leaders, who knew how to please God, or the astrologers, who studied the planets and how they influenced human events.

If people did consult a doctor, however, Sources 4–6 show what they might have expected.

SOURCE 3 A letter to Francesco Datini from his friend Ser Lapo Mazzei

66 *I have seen two of my children die in my arms, in a few hours. God knows how great my hopes were for the eldest. And God knows that, for many years, he never failed to say his daily prayers, in the morning and even on his knees in his room. He said he was called to judgement and ready to obey.*

Francesco, take courage and trust in God. Fear not, for if you put your hopes in him, he will not fail you. Comfort your wife and she you. Loosen your spirit a little from these worldly possessions.

Please help look after my family if I, too, must leave this mockery of life, for indeed it is a mockery and there is little difference between life and death. 99

SOURCE 4 Written in the fourteenth century by the poet Petrarch

66 *After lengthy discussions the doctors announced that I would be dead by midnight. They said that the only remedy would be to draw some cords tightly around me, to stop me sleeping. Their orders were not carried out, for I have always told my servants not to do what doctors command. Indeed, do just the opposite. I spent the night in a deep, sweet sleep. I who was meant to die at midnight was discovered by the doctors, when they came on the next day, writing.* 99

DID HEALTH AND MEDICINE IMPROVE?

SOURCE 5 A story from the fifteenth century, quoted in *The Florentine Renaissance* by Vincent Cronin

One day doctors sent the Bishop a new medicine. He emptied the medicine into his chamber pot. Next day the doctors found him better and said how foolish he had been to refuse medicine for so long.

'Your medicines are indeed marvellous,' said the Bishop, 'for by just putting them under my bed I have recovered. Had I swallowed them, I should have become immortal.'

SOURCE 6 Around 1400 Margherita Datini was given the following prescription by her doctors. Her illness was probably malaria. The 'Hail Mary' and 'Our Father' are special prayers said by Christians

Let three sage leaves be picked in the morning before sunrise. Let the man who picks them be kneeling, saying three 'Hail Marys' (in honour of God and the Holy Trinity). Then send the leaves here in a letter, and I will write words on each.

As the fever approaches, let her say an 'Our Father' and a 'Hail Mary', and then eat a leaf, and so for each one of the three. When she is done with eating them, she will be rid of the fever. But she must have faith, for if she has not, they will be of no help.

Through the fifteenth and sixteenth centuries hospitals were built in Florence. A hospital was established in 1445 which was paid for by charging on goods brought into the town. One hundred years later a British visitor to Florence wrote about the city's facilities (Source 7).

SOURCE 7 Written by William Thomas in the sixteenth century

They have many good hospitals for the relief of the sick and the poor. They receive a great number of men and women, but into separate buildings. There they are given good treatment and their beds, their sheets, and every other thing is so clean, that honest men and women are not ashamed to go there for treatment.

The Santa Maria Nuova hospital alone may dispense yearly more than 20,000 crowns. For that reason they have excellent physicians, good apothecaries [who make drugs], keen ministers and every other thing necessary.

1. What attitudes do Sources 4 and 5 show to the advice of doctors?
2. Is there any evidence in Sources 4–6 that the remedies proposed by doctors were likely to be helpful?
3. Using the information on the last three pages, make a list of ways in which a) the understanding of disease b) the treatment of the sick c) the attitude to doctors had changed or not changed during the period of the Renaissance.

Changing ideas about anatomy

Throughout the Middle Ages the most important book about medicine was a classical text which had been written in the second century AD by Claudius Galen. Galen was a Greek doctor who had treated the Roman Emperor successfully. He became the most respected doctor in the Empire.

As we have already seen, the ancient Greeks and Romans found out about the world by observation. Galen's knowledge of the human body was based on DISSECTING corpses – and recording what he saw. However, in Galen's time the dissection of human corpses was forbidden for religious reasons, so most of the time he used the bodies of animals to investigate how the human body worked.

1. What problems might Galen have had in using animals to learn about the human body?

Galen was fairly accurate in many of his descriptions of how the body worked. He was taken as the great authority throughout the Middle Ages and well into the Renaissance. His works were the main textbooks at medical schools for 1400 years after his death. Many of the remedies he suggested were useful. For example, doctors treating Lorenzo de' Medici learned from Galen how SPA waters could be used to treat Lorenzo's gout and kidney and liver troubles. They suggested he should bathe in and drink the waters from spas around Tuscany, which were rich in minerals. Lorenzo's pain was relieved by this

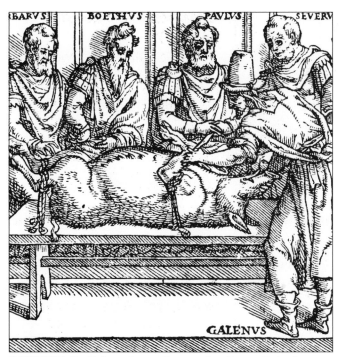

SOURCE 8 Galen dissecting a pig. From Galen's *Collected Works*, published in Venice in AD 1556

out if there was any physical explanation for their crimes. A book was published containing the notes of twenty such post-mortems.

Even the Church began to allow dissection – but only as a way of proving that Galen was right! You can see how a fifteenth-century doctor would teach about the human body from Source 9.

As in other areas of life, however, the Renaissance was a time for rediscovering the critical attitude of the great classical scholars. The new Renaissance attitudes emerging in Italy began to make it possible to observe the human body more closely than Galen had ever been able to do.

As dissection became more acceptable and commonplace artists began to investigate the structure of human muscles by dissection. Leonardo da Vinci was the first to make truly exact anatomical drawings (see page 17).

SOURCE 9 Mondino de Luzzi teaching about the human body.

treatment and he visited the spas regularly throughout his life.

However, there were other reasons why Galen's works remained the main textbooks for so many centuries. Throughout the Middle Ages the Church discouraged new ideas. They believed that scholars should instead devote their time to teaching and explaining old ideas.

They still did not allow the dissection of human corpses, so there was no way for scholars in the Christian world to test Galen's theories. One scholar working in an Islamic country showed up some of the mistakes in Galen's works as early as the thirteenth century. But his ideas either never reached the Christian world, or if they did they were rejected because they went against the teaching of Galen. In any case the Christian scholars would have had no way of confirming or challenging them because dissection was still forbidden by the Church.

By the time of the fifteenth century, however, the rules about dissection were being relaxed. In June 1348 – during an outbreak of the plague – the rulers of Florence had allowed surgeons to do POST-MORTEMS on plague victims. However, they were not doing this in order to find out the cause of the plague. Instead they were dissecting the corpses of criminals to find

Andreas Vesalius

The new interest in ANATOMY allowed people to question Galen. The person who did this with the most important results was Andreas Vesalius.

Andreas Vesalius (1514–64) was one of the great medical men of the Renaissance. He was born in Brussels (in modern-day Belgium). His father was a doctor and Andreas followed him in his profession. He was so keen to learn about the human body that he stole parts of the body of a criminal from the gallows on the walls outside Louvain where he was studying as a medical student.

In 1537 he moved to Italy. He became Professor of Anatomy at Padua University.

At this time the Catholic Church was just beginning to realise that some of the new medical discoveries were going against traditional ideas and was trying to clamp down. However, Padua was part of the Republic of Venice and was famous for having greater freedom from the Church than other areas of Italy.

Vesalius spent six years in Padua and was able to obtain bodies for DISSECTION from the city law courts where the bodies of executed criminals were handed over to him.

He wrote a book called *The Fabric of the Human Body*. It was published in 1543 when he was only 29 years old and became widely available. Vesalius said he wanted his book to be an atlas of the human body.

Vesalius' careful research led him to believe that Galen was wrong about many details of anatomy. He was not the first to say this, but he was the first to be able to back up his criticisms of Galen with evidence from his own dissections, and to explain why Galen was wrong. See Source 11, for example.

SOURCE 10
Vesalius conducting an anatomy lesson. From the title page of his *Fabric of the Human Body*, 1543

SOURCE 11 Written by Vesalius in his *Fabric of the Human Body*

"The jaw of most animals is formed of two bones joined together at the chin where the lower jaw ends in a point. In man, however, the lower jaw is formed of a single bone.

Nevertheless, Galen and most of the skilled doctors assert that the jaw is not a single bone. In spite of this, no human jaw has yet come to my attention which is made of two bones."

Vesalius' criticisms were very controversial. Galen's reputation was so great that he was bitterly attacked for disagreeing with him. In many universities Vesalius' ideas were officially banned for another fifty years.

It's strange that in many ways Vesalius was using exactly the same method of enquiry – detailed observation – that Galen had used to reach his own conclusions. If the classical interest in the natural world had continued through the Middle Ages, then the flaws in Galen's ideas might have been spotted much earlier. But no-one had been allowed to challenge these ideas for centuries, so when Renaissance scholars finally provided evidence for the mistakes, their findings came as a shock to people who had been taught not to question traditional knowledge.

Vesalius had used scientific methods, however. And those professors of anatomy who were influenced by Renaissance ideas soon began to teach from Vesalius' books, and copy his methods. Over the next century they made many important new discoveries about such things as the structure of the human heart. Dissection, observation and experiment became the accepted way of improving medical knowledge. Doctors all over Europe conducted experiments – including some gruesome ones such as that described in Source 12.

SOURCE 12 From a medical treatise by Amboise Paré, 1585. He had been asked by the King of France to judge on whether a traditional ANTIDOTE to poison – the Bezoar – would work

"It was an easy matter to try out the Bezoar on people condemned to be hanged. A cook was brought who was to have been hanged for stealing two silver dishes. The King asked him if he would take poison on the condition that if the Bezoar antidote worked then he should be allowed to live. The cook answered that he was willing to take the risk.

The poison was given to him and then, immediately after the poison, some of the Bezoar.

An hour later I found him lying on the ground like a beast, his tongue out, his eyes fiery, vomiting and with blood flowing out of his ears, nose and mouth. At length he died in great torment. I opened his body and found the bottom of his stomach as dry as if it had been burnt."

Activity

Compare Source 10 with Source 9 on page 43. Make a list of the differences and similarities between de Luzzi's lesson and Vesalius' lesson.

Now, with a partner, make up a conversation between the two doctors about anatomy. They may discuss:

■ how each knows about the composition of the human body

■ how each teaches anatomy to his students.

1. Why do you think the doctors and professors did not accept Vesalius' new ideas? Was it because:
a) they were stupid
b) they did not want to change the ways in which they had been doing things for years
c) they had not heard about Vesalius' discoveries
d) they knew about them and had studied them, but did not think they were right; or was it for
e) some other reason?
   Explain your answer.
2. Make a list of factors which explain why the understanding of anatomy improved in Italy at this time.
3. In what ways is the experiment described in Source 12 similar to/different from the methods of Vesalius?

Was the Earth the centre of the universe?

IN the Middle Ages people were very interested in the stars and planets. ASTROLOGERS studied the planets keenly because they believed that they had an influence on people's lives. They argued that if they knew what the planets were doing, then they could work out how those movements would affect people on the Earth.

During the Renaissance, however, a new science known as ASTRONOMY emerged. Astronomers' main aim was to study the movement of the stars and planets scientifically and so build up a more accurate picture of what the universe was like. Just as Leonardo encouraged painters to observe the natural world around them, so astronomers wanted to observe the world of the universe above them.

When Renaissance scientists looked at the writings of the ancient Greeks, they found the view of the universe in Source 1. Over the period of the Renaissance this view of the universe was tested and challenged by astronomers and scientists all over Europe. We are going to follow this story through the work of four Renaissance scientists.

The Renaissance view of the universe

Nicolaus Copernicus (1473–1543)
Copernicus was born in Poland. He came to Italy to study Greek, mathematics, astronomy and medicine.

He did not have advanced telescopes to observe the stars but, basing his work on logic and geometric calculation, he decided that the Earth, other planets and stars revolved in circles around the Sun.

He published these ideas in a book called *The Revolution of the Celestial Spheres* in 1543, the same year in which Vesalius published his treatise on human anatomy (see page 44).

Tycho Brahe (1546–1601)
He was a Danish astronomer who set up an observatory to carefully watch and plot the movements of the stars. Even so, he still supported Ptolemy's view that the Earth was at the centre of the universe.

Johann Kepler (1571–1630)
Kepler was a German astronomer who worked in Tycho Brahe's observatory. He used mathematical

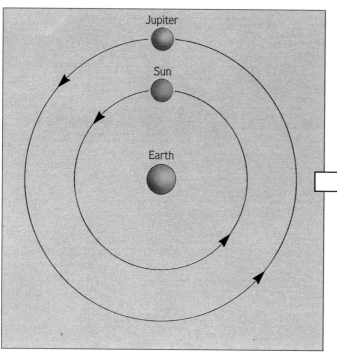

SOURCE 1 Diagram showing the ancient Greek and Roman view of the universe. This theory of the universe was supported by the Christian Church. Can you think why?

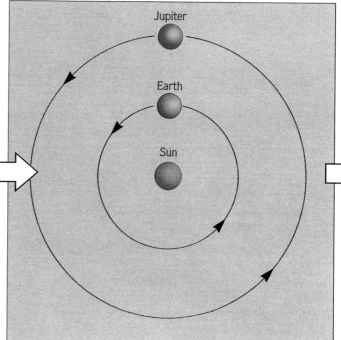

SOURCE 2 Diagram showing Copernicus' theories about the universe

calculations to work out how the planets moved. These proved Copernicus' theory that the Sun was at the centre of the universe. But he realised that in one aspect Copernicus had been wrong. He proved that the planets travelled round the Sun in elliptical, not circular orbits (See Source 3 below). Kepler's ideas challenged the Church's teaching and he was expelled from his university.

1. Make a list of new things Copernicus, Brahe and Kepler discovered about the universe.
2. Which ideas from classical times did some of them keep?
3. What does this tell us about the way ideas change through time?

▶ Johann Kepler

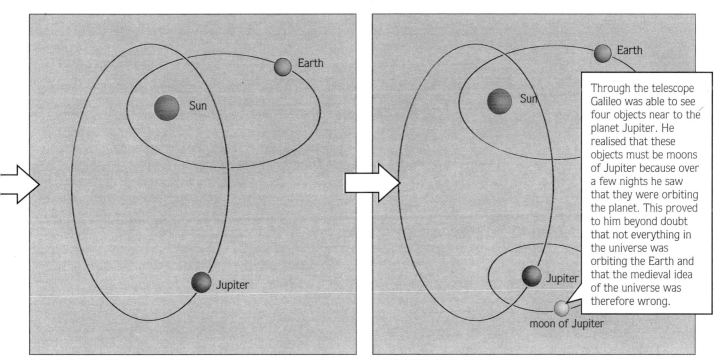

SOURCE 3 Diagram of Kepler's planetary model

SOURCE 4 Galileo's theories about the universe

Through the telescope Galileo was able to see four objects near to the planet Jupiter. He realised that these objects must be moons of Jupiter because over a few nights he saw that they were orbiting the planet. This proved to him beyond doubt that not everything in the universe was orbiting the Earth and that the medieval idea of the universe was therefore wrong.

WAS THE EARTH THE CENTRE OF THE UNIVERSE?

Galileo Galilei (1564–1642)
Galileo was born in Pisa, Italy. He studied mathematics and physics and in 1589 became a lecturer in mathematics at the University of Pisa.

Galileo's main interest was astronomy. He knew that to really understand the universe he needed a more powerful telescope. When in 1609 he heard about a telescope made by a Dutch scientist, Lippershey (modelled on lenses designed by Arab astronomers in the eighth century), he copied it, improved it and made important new observations that proved decisively that Copernicus and Kepler were right (see Source 4).

By now the Church was very worried by the new theories about the universe. It banned Copernicus' book in 1616 and tried to stop Galileo's work. Eventually he agreed not to write any more about his discoveries. However, the silencing of Galileo came too late, because Renaissance theories about the universe were by then being accepted by scientists all over Europe.

Activity
Draw a timeline from 1450 to 1700 and mark on it
■ the names of the people whose work is described in this section
■ their discoveries or inventions which added to our knowledge of the universe.
You may ask your teacher for an outline to help you.

Galileo at work

Galileo made a number of other important scientific discoveries. We are going to investigate two examples which show both how a Renaissance scientist worked and also how such discoveries could be useful.

The law of falling bodies
One of Galileo's greatest contributions to modern science was his 'law of falling bodies', which he proved in 1604. Suppose you dropped two stones – a large one, and a small one of the same shape – from the same height. Which would reach the ground first? It is tempting to think that the big stone would be pulled by a greater force and therefore hit the ground first. But this idea would be wrong, as Galileo proved. There is a story that Galileo dropped two cannon-balls of different weights off the Leaning Tower of Pisa. They hit the ground at the same time because,

although the shape of an object affects how fast it falls (because of friction between the object and the air in the atmosphere), its weight does not.

Galileo proved his 'law of falling bodies', but he could not explain *why* the objects hit the ground at the same time. However, he had laid a foundation for others to build on. Over seventy years later, in 1679, the English scientist Isaac Newton explained that the reason this happened was that the earth pulls all objects towards it with the same force. He called this force 'gravity'.

The ideal place to prove Galileo's theory would be on the moon where there is no atmosphere to interfere. So, during one of the American moon landings in the 1970s, one of the astronauts dropped a hammer and a feather on to the surface of the moon. They both hit the ground at the same time. Galileo was right.

---

1. Add Galileo's discovery and the work of Isaac Newton to your timeline.

The pendulum clock
Galileo was very interested in PENDULUMS. In the cathedral at Pisa there was an enormous incense burner that hung from the centre of the ceiling. The story goes that, when sitting in church, Galileo used to watch the incense burner as it swang from side to side. However long the swing, it always seemed to take the same amount of time. Or did it?

Galileo set up an experiment to find out if this was right (see Source 5). He knew that the ancient Greek scientist Aristotle had said that when a pendulum swung, the long swing (A) took longer than the short swing (B). Galileo proved by his experiment that large and small swings took the same time.

Galileo had showed that the weight of the pendulum or the length of the swing was not important. What determined how long each swing took was the length of the piece of string holding the pendulum. This discovery had an immediate usefulness for clock-makers, who were experimenting with pendulum clocks. Each swing of the pendulum had to take precisely one second. Using Galileo's discovery, clock-makers could now make much more accurate clocks, because all they had to do to make a clock tick faster or more slowly was to raise or lower the pendulum. The pendulum clock remained one of the most reliable time-keeping devices until well into the twentieth century.

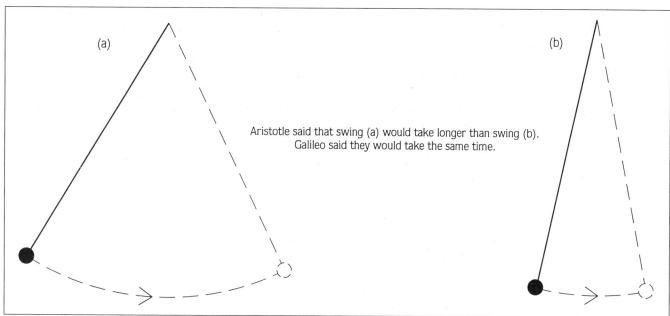

(a)

(b)

Aristotle said that swing (a) would take longer than swing (b).
Galileo said they would take the same time.

SOURCE 5 The movement of a pendulum

Activity

Galileo showed that the time it takes for a pendulum to swing backwards and forwards does not depend on its weight. You can do the following experiment to prove it.

Work in pairs. You will need a weight on a piece of string and a stop-watch.

1. One person holds the top of the string so that it remains at the same height. Measure the length of the string. The other starts the 'pendulum' on a small swing as in picture B in Source 5. Count the number of swings in thirty seconds. How long does each swing take?

   Now repeat the above, but start the pendulum on a long swing as in A in Source 5. Count the number of swings. How long does each swing take?

   Record your conclusions on a chart like this:

Length of string	Weight of pendulum	Number of swings	Time of swing

2. Now repeat the experiment a number of times using longer or shorter string (it doesn't matter which) and lighter or heavier weights for the 'pendulum'.
3. Which of the following factors determines the time of the swing – the length of the string, the weight of the pendulum or the length of the swing?

1. ■ 'People who make scientific discoveries are building on the work of scientists through history'. Write one or two paragraphs explaining whether you agree or disagree with this statement. Support your answer by referring to the case studies on the last four pages and your timeline.

Was there a Renaissance in other parts of Europe?

So far in this book we have mainly been studying events in Italy. In the next few pages we are going to examine similar changes which were taking place elsewhere, particularly in Northern Europe.

North European painting

During the fifteenth and sixteenth centuries there were great changes in painting in Northern Europe. Look at Sources 1 and 2. They were both painted by North European artists.

▲**SOURCE 1** *Christ in the house of Simon the Pharisee* by a Netherlands artist, Dieric Bouts (1420–75)

SOURCE 2 Self-portrait by the Netherlands artist Marten van Heemskerck, 1537. Van Heemskerck visited Italy in the 1530s. He met the famous architect Vasari and made drawings of ancient Roman and Renaissance buildings

1. Look carefully at Sources 1 and 2. What evidence is there in these paintings that the artists had visited Italy? (You may need to refer back to page 24).

Case study: Pieter Breugel the Elder

One of the greatest artists of the Northern Renaissance was Pieter Breugel (1528–69), who lived in Flanders (modern-day Belgium) in the town of Antwerp for the first part of his life. As a young man he travelled in Italy, then settled in Brussels in 1563, where he lived and worked until he died. He is sometimes called Pieter Breugel the Elder, to distinguish him from his son Pieter who was also an artist.

During Breugel's lifetime Flanders was ruled by Spain. There were frequent revolts by the Flemish people against their Spanish rulers, but these were put down very harshly.

Breugel was a well-educated man but came to be known as 'Peasant Breugel' because he was fascinated by the lives of the peasants he met and observed in the villages of Flanders.

Breugel's paintings such as Sources 3 and 4 give us a picture of the lives of the ordinary people doing their everyday work or celebrating special occasions such as weddings. They were based on careful observation of the peasants' lives – of the way they dressed, of the houses they lived in. However, Breugel also used his paintings to tell Bible stories or moral tales about the sins of gluttony and drunkenness.

◄**SOURCE 3** *The Peasant Wedding Feast* by Pieter Breugel the Elder

▼**SOURCE 4** *The Massacre of the Innocents* by Pieter Breugel the Elder. It shows an event described in the Bible. When Jesus Christ was born, King Herod felt so threatened by the birth of a new 'king' that he had all children under the age of one year killed

SOURCE 5 Adapted from a book by an art historian, Max J. Friedlander, written in the 1950s

66*Peasant Breugel was the first to observe the daily round of human activity with honesty, humour and without mockery or bias.*

*During his lifetime Breugel's paintings appealed mainly to the man in the street – more for the stories they told than for their artistic value. He instructed, delighted and entertained people.*99

Activity

1. Imagine you are Bruegel and write a letter to an Italian artist, explaining what you are trying to achieve in your paintings.
2. Using Sources 3 and 4 to help you, choose a Bible story which you know and say how you think Bruegel would have painted it. Include details of the building where the scene might take place, the clothing of the people, and any tools or furnishings in the picture.

1. Look at Source 3. What does this painting tell us about the lives of the peasants in the picture?
2. Look at Source 4. This shows a story which is supposed to have taken place in the first century AD in Palestine. Where does Breugel show it taking place? Give reasons for your answer.
3. Why do you think Breugel chose this story for one of his pictures? You may need to refer back to the background information about Flanders.
4. In what ways are Breugel's paintings useful as sources of evidence about the lives of Flemish people in the sixteenth century?
5. Read Source 5. Could this description be used of any of the Italian artists you have studied?

WAS THERE A RENAISSANCE IN OTHER PARTS OF EUROPE?

Developments in Northern Europe

1430	Flemish artist Jan van Eyck perfects the use of oil paints
1450	German printer Johann Gutenberg sets up first European printing press in Mainz
1486	French musician Josquin des Prés writes Renaissance music
1498	German painter and engraver Albrecht Dürer makes illustrations for book *Apocalypse*
1521	German monk Martin Luther and his followers become Protestants
1530	Netherlands artist Marten van Heemskerck visits Italy and draws the ruins of Rome
1533	German artist Hans Holbein becomes court painter to Henry VIII of England
1533/34	French writer Rabelais writes *Pantagruel* and *Gargantua*
1543	Polish astronomer Copernicus publishes *The Revolution of the Celestial Spheres*
1560	Flemish artist Pieter Breugel the Elder paints scenes from peasant life
1590	English playwright William Shakespeare begins writing plays
1605	Spanish writer Cervantes writes *Don Quixote*
1609	German astronomer Johann Kepler writes *New Astronomy*

SOURCE 6 Adapted from Peter Burke's *The Italian Renaissance*, 1987

66 ■ ... *northern or western Europeans are generally held to have surpassed their Italian masters in writing stories. The great masters of this were Rabelais (French), Cervantes (Spanish), and Sir Philip Sidney (English).*
■ *In music the Netherlands was recognised as pre-eminent, even by Italians.* 99

▶ **SOURCE 7** A woodcut by the German artist Albrecht Dürer. The woodcut was a spin-off from printing, and a form of art in which the North Europeans excelled. What do you think is happening in the picture?

1. Compare the timeline above with the upper part of the timeline on pages 4–5. Would you say that the Renaissance outside Italy was happening, before, at the same time as, or after the Italian Renaissance?
2. Would you say it was concerned with the same or different subjects?

Two-way traffic

Although there were differences between the Renaissance in Italy and that in Northern and Western Europe, influences went in both directions. North Europeans visited Italy in increasing numbers through the fifteenth and sixteenth centuries to study law, architecture, ANATOMY, Latin and astronomy as well as painting.

At the same time as other Europeans were visiting and learning from Italy, Italian artists, writers and craftsmen were travelling to other parts of Europe. They were much in demand. The King of France brought Italian architects, sculptors and goldsmiths to work for him. Other Renaissance artists worked in Spain and Poland, and some came to work for Henry VII and VIII in England.

One Flemish artist, Jan van Eyck, working in the 1430s, greatly influenced the development of Italian art. He had begun to include background landscapes to his great ALTARPIECES (see Source 8). Italian artists were so impressed by his feeling for landscape and his skill in oil painting, that they took the ideas back to Italy where they were quickly adopted.

Activity

Work with a partner.
   Look back through this book to find other examples of any of the following:
a) people from other countries coming to Italy to learn from the Italians
b) people in Italy getting ideas from others outside Italy
c) people from Italy going to other countries to practise their work.
   As a start, you might look at pages 32, 30 and 18.

1. Use the timeline and Sources 1–8 to make a list of ways in which the Renaissance in Northern and Western Europe was a) similar to
   b) different from the Italian Renaissance. Together as a class use your ideas to make two large charts – one showing the differences and the other the similarities.

SOURCE 8 Section of the *Ghent altarpiece* by van Eyck

Would the Renaissance have spread without the printing press?

WE have seen that a new interest in the art and ideas of the classical world began at least as early as the fourteenth century. Some historians say that it was not the first time that this had happened and that during the Middle Ages scholars in Italy had been keen to study their classical past. So other 'mini-renaissances' had taken place in the ninth and twelfth centuries.

The Renaissance of the fourteenth and fifteenth centuries, however, was different because it affected the whole of Italy and its ideas spread during the next century to affect most of Europe.

Why did this happen? We are going to look at one factor which may have played an important part in the spread of the Renaissance – the invention of the printing press in the fifteenth century. Would the Renaissance have had the impact it did without this invention?

Handwritten books

During the Middle Ages books were written by hand, usually by monks working in monasteries (see Source 4 on page 6). The books were carefully written, decorated and bound. They were very valuable and some books were chained to the shelves to keep them safe. You can still see a chained medieval library in Hereford Cathedral.

---

1. Use Sources 1 and 2 to help you list some of the problems of producing books by this method.

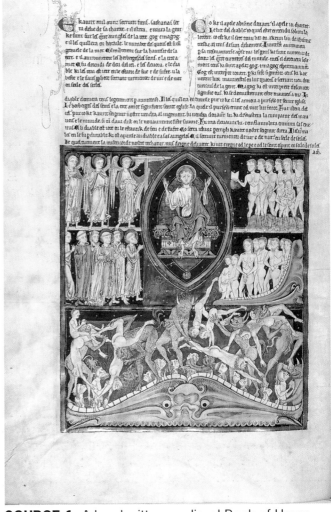

SOURCE 1 A handwritten medieval Book of Hours

SOURCE 2 The library of Hereford Cathedral

Paper-making

Before the invention of paper, people had written on specially treated sheep and goat skins. The skin was soaked, scraped and then made smooth by rubbing with PUMICE STONE. This was called parchment. Very thin parchment made from animals with fine skins such as lambs or calves was called vellum. This tended to be used for small books.

Paper was first invented by the Chinese in about AD 105. A young Chinese named Tsai Lun made paper by mixing plant fibres, old rags, fishing nets and hemp (a tough fibre used for making rope) with water and beating them to a fine paste. He then poured the mixture into a sieve with a wooden frame, the size of a sheet of paper. The water drained away and what was left, when dried, became paper. The Muslim world could see how useful paper could be and learned the secrets of making it from the Chinese. By the twelfth century this knowledge had reached Europe.

Block printing

Block printing had been invented by the Chinese in the seventh century AD. Blocks of wood, the size of a page, were carved with pictures and writing, in the same way as lino- or woodcuts are done today. Ink was then put on to the block.

A sheet of paper was then laid on the block and the back of the paper was rubbed with a pad. The paper used for this type of printing was very soft and absorbed ink easily, therefore it was only possible to use one side of it.

A new block had to be cut for each page, since the letters could not be moved around. Block printing was only really useful for books with few pages and where many copies were needed. It was also used for printing pictures and playing cards.

Block printing was introduced to Europe in the fourteenth century. Blocks may have been brought from China by travellers, but it is thought that the idea came with the craze for card games. Block-printed cards were at first imported from China.

Activity

Imagine you are a printer living in Europe in the fifteenth century. You currently use the method of block printing, but you want to improve your methods. You are aware of the developments shown in the pictures. How could each one improve your printing?

A block printer replacing a broken letter in the block

A jeweller putting letters on to a bracelet, using a punch

A winemaker using a wine press to press grapes

Movable type

The Chinese were the first to invent movable type in the eleventh century. Movable type consisted of separate letters which were put into a frame to make words and sentences. The letters could be removed from the frame and re-set to create other pages. The first single movable letters were made from baked clay. Metal type was introduced in about 1300, but movable type did not yet spread to Europe.

Johann Gutenberg

Movable type and the method of printing using a press were invented in Europe by Johann Gutenberg. He was a merchant and goldsmith from Mainz in Germany and he set up the first printing press there in 1450. The money to develop the invention was provided by Johann Fust, a wealthy goldsmith from Mainz.

One of the first books to be printed on a press was a Latin Bible. It consisted of 641 leaves. Each page had two columns of print with 42 lines to each page. It was the first large book to be printed. Some copies were sold in Paris for 50 crowns each. This was very cheap, since handwritten copies sold at 500 crowns each.

Soon printing presses were being established all over Europe. Two German churchmen set up the first printing press in Italy at a monastery near Rome in 1465. Within two years they had moved their press into Rome itself. By 1500 there were well over a hundred presses in Italy.

SOURCE 3 A printing shop. An engraving made in 1598

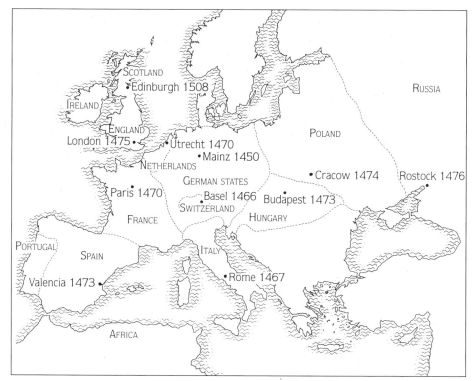
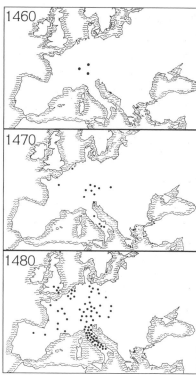

SOURCE 4 Maps to show when and where printing presses were established

Activity

1. Look at Source 3. Match the features labelled A–G with the following descriptions:
   - Master who owns the printing shop
   - Compositors setting up the type
   - Paper being delivered
   - Inking the type
   - Printer using press
   - Printed pages hung up to dry
   - A young apprentice
2. What does the information on the maps in Source 4 tell you about the spread of the printing press through Europe?
3. Make two lists: one of groups of people whom you might expect to welcome the printing press; the other of groups whom you might expect to oppose it.

The impact of the printing press

The first large printed book was a Bible and printing was immediately put to use to spread religious ideas around Europe. But how important was it in spreading the new Renaissance ideas about art, architecture and music, the study of the ideas of the classical world and the Greek and Latin languages? Here are two viewpoints:

SOURCE 5 From V.H.H. Green, *Renaissance and Reformation*, 1982

❝ *The Aldine Press at Venice did more than anything else to spread the values of the Italian Renaissance.* ❞

SOURCE 6 Adapted from the *New Cambridge Modern History*, 1956

❝ *The printing press took many generations to affect men in any definite way. The printed book did not produce important changes in what people liked or thought.* ❞

1. How do Sources 5 and 6 differ in their view of the importance of the printing press?
2. Do they agree about anything?

One way of examining the impact of the printing press is to look at what kinds of books were first printed. We have already seen that the Bible was the first printed book. Sources 7–11 describe and illustrate a number of other books printed in the fifteenth century.

The Aldine Press – the most famous Italian printing house – was set up by Aldus Manutius. Its aim was to print texts in classical languages, such as scientific works by Aristotle and poems by Virgil.

Italian printers developed new TYPEFACES. The German printers had used 'Gothic' print which looked like the handwriting of monks. The Italian printers developed 'Roman' type which was easier to read. It is still popular today.

𝕬𝕭𝕮𝕯𝕰𝕱𝕲𝕳𝕴𝕵𝕶𝕷𝕸
𝖆𝖇𝖈𝖉𝖊𝖋𝖌𝖍𝖎𝖏𝖐𝖑𝖒

ABCDEFGHIJKLM
abcdefghijklm

SOURCE 7 Examples of Gothic and Roman type

Most Aldine books were written in Latin or Greek, but an increasing number of books from other presses were written in the native language of the country.

Printers' lists and library catalogues of early printed books suggest that Bibles, prayer books, religious writings, history books and stories were more likely to be printed than classical texts.

SOURCE 8 The contents of the library of two Florentine sculptors who owned 29 books between them (analysed by Peter Burke in *The Italian Renaissance*, 1987)

❝ ■ *More than half the books were religious; among them a Bible, A Life of Saint Jerome and a book describing the miracles of Mary, the mother of Jesus.*

■ *Among the SECULAR (non-religious) books there were two favourite Florentine poets – Dante and Boccaccio – as well as a history of Florence.*

■ *Classical literature was represented by a Life of the ancient ruler Alexander the Great and a history of Rome by Livy.* ❞

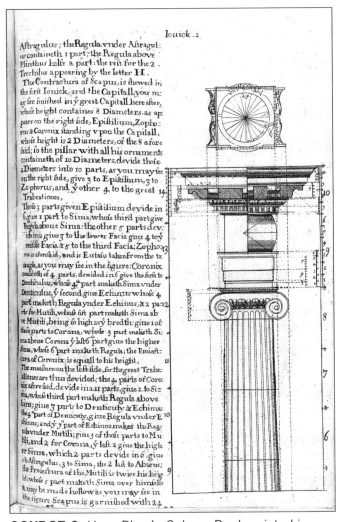

SOURCE 9 Hans Blum's *Column Book*, printed in English. Hans Blum was a Renaissance architect

1. Make a list of subjects covered by early printed books from the information and sources on these two pages.
2. What evidence is there that printing presses still concentrated on ideas from the Middle Ages?
3. What evidence is there that they helped spread Renaissance ideas?
4. Look back to pages 44 and 46, where two famous books were mentioned. How important do you think the printing press was in spreading the ideas in these books?

Here endith the squyers prologue
And here begynneth his Tale

a   T surrye in the londe of Tartary
There duelled a king that warred ruffy
Throught whiche they dyed many a doughty man

SOURCE 10 Five lines and a woodcut from Chaucer's *Canterbury Tales*, printed in English (London, 1492). Chaucer was an English medieval writer

SOURCE 11 Aesop's FABLES – printed in English (London, 1484). Aesop was an ancient Greek writer

no drede ne fere no thynge/ For I shalle not accuse the/ For I shalle skewe to hym another way/ And as the hunter came/ he demaunded of the shepherd yf he had sene the wulf pass

SOURCE 12 Books printed in Europe by 1500

religious 45%
literary 30%
legal 10%
science 10%
other 5%

Activity

Below are six ways ideas could have spread round Europe during the Renaissance.

a) A pilgrim from England travelling to Rome in 1500
b) Merchants travelling from Florence to other parts of Europe to sell cloth in 1480
c) An Italian sculptor working on the tomb of the English king, Henry VII, in Westminster Abbey in 1512
d) The printing presses of Venice which had printed 3,000 book titles by 1500
e) A soldier in the army of the French king, Charles VIII, who invaded Milan in 1485
f) The Venetian ambassador visiting the court of the English king, Henry VIII, in 1520

1. On the sheet supplied by your teacher indicate whether each of these was very important, quite important or less important.
2. Write between one and three paragraphs with the title 'Would the ideas of the Renaissance have spread without the invention of the printing press?'

Why did the Renaissance start in Italy?

In the past 54 pages we have examined various aspects of the Renaissance in detail. We have focused particularly on four areas of change – art, architecture, medicine and science – which were particularly important in the Renaissance.

However, you can see from the timeline on pages 4–5 that there were many other new developments in Europe at this time. New styles of literature emerged. European explorers sailed round the world and landed in America for the first time. And in much of Northern Europe a new Protestant Church broke away from the Roman Catholic Church, bringing about major changes in religious life.

Historians generally agree that this period from the fourteenth to the sixteenth century was an important turning point. What they disagree about is what caused the changes, and in particular why so many of them began in Italy.

On these two pages we review some of the factors which historians say made the Renaissance start where and when it did.

---

1. Choose one statement 'for' and one 'against' from each box and find evidence in this book to support each one.
2. Choose one factor which you think is particularly important and write a paragraph explaining your choice.

Because . . . changes were taking place in the Church

For:
- In the Middle Ages the Church had supported traditional ideas. In the fourteenth and fifteenth centuries some parts of the Church began to allow new ideas to develop
- People became less obsessed with heaven and hell and more interested in the natural world around them
- The Church no longer provided all education. Some secular schools were set up

Against:
- When it became clear that new ideas would weaken the position of the Church, its leaders actually tried to ban them
- Most Italians - even the leading figures of the Renaissance - still seemed to believe in heaven and hell

Because . . . new inventions made scientific progress possible

For:
- The invention of the telescope allowed astronomers to see the planets and stars more clearly
- New printing technology led to new ideas being spread much more quickly

Against:
- The improved telescope was not developed in Italy but in Holland, and anyway it was based on earlier work done by Arab scientists
- Printing was not pioneered in Italy; the Italians learned it from the Germans

Because . . . ancient Greek and Roman ideas were rediscovered

For:
■ From 1300 ancient manuscripts were being rediscovered and people in Italy found out more about the ideas of scholars in ancient Rome and Greece
■ The people of Italy were inspired by the physical remains of the Roman Empire they found around them
■ Architects copied and learned from the engineering achievements of the ancient Romans and Greeks

Against:
■ Many of the classical manuscripts had never actually been lost, in fact the ancient manuscripts were part of the problem — Galen's books were accepted uncritically for centuries, and held back medical progress
■ The physical remains of the Roman Empire had been there for centuries but hadn't inspired a Renaissance earlier

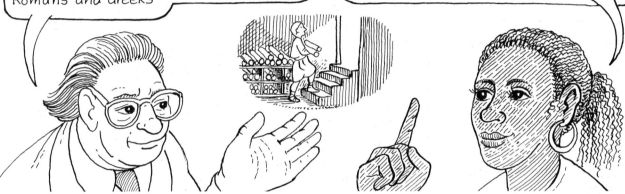

Because . . . Italy was richer than other European countries

For:
■ Wealthy merchants and governments in Italy had money to spend on art and new buildings
■ Many rich people began to support new artists, scholars or scientists
■ It also became fashionable for the children of rich families to be educated in new ideas, and education was no longer controlled only by the Church
■ Becoming wealthy gave rich people less need to work, and more time to think about new ideas
■ Italians wanted Renaissance Italy to be as great as the Roman Empire had been

Against:
■ Trading and banking profits were often spent purely on war and defence, not on art and science
■ Only a very small number of rich people – and very few women – were educated
■ The great increase in Italy's wealth began centuries before the Renaissance really got going

What has the Renaissance given us?

THE legacy of the Renaissance can be seen all around us today. Here are a few of the areas of life in which its influence can still be seen.

■ Education. Before the Renaissance all education was in the hands of the Church. Since that time most education has been SECULAR and has taught pupils about the world around them as well as about religion.

■ Science. The Renaissance began the approach to science that nowadays we think of as normal – where you do experiments to find out the truth.

■ Architecture. Many of the styles of building developed during the Renaissance period are still popular today. You can probably find examples near your home or school which copy the Renaissance ideas on page 32.

SUPERMARKET

■ Tourism. The fame of Renaissance cities such as Florence, Venice or Rome still attracts millions of people to visit them every year. Many millions of pounds have been spent on preserving and restoring works of art such as the ceiling of the Sistine Chapel.

LEONARDO EXHIBITION

1. Find one other feature of the Renaissance – from this book or from your own knowledge or research – which has had an effect on our lives today. Use drawings and your own words to explain how this aspect of the Renaissance influences people's lives in the twentieth century.

■ ARCHAEOLOGY. The study of ancient remains which interested the scholars of the Renaissance continues to this day. Many of our museums are still full of the kind of objects which fascinated the people of that time.

Activity

You are the curator of a museum and have been asked to put on an exhibition called 'Images of the Renaissance'.

1. Select four pictures from this book which you think show something important about the Renaissance.
2. Write a description of each image to go in a catalogue of the exhibition.
3. Write an introduction for the catalogue explaining why you chose each of the four images.

Design a cover for your exhibition catalogue and include it in a class display.

Glossary

altarpiece   a religious painting placed behind the altar in a church
anatomy   the scientific study of the structure of the body
antidote   medicine given to reverse the effects of poison
apprentice   learner of an art, craft or trade who works with an expert for a number of years (often seven)
archaeology   study of the past often by digging up remains which have been left behind, such as buildings, pottery and tools
artillery   guns and cannons
astrologer   person who studies the effects of the stars and planets on human beings
astronomy   the science of the study of space including the planets and stars

brocade   silk fabric with a raised pattern woven into it
bronze   brown-coloured metal made mainly of copper and tin

chancellor   an important state official
Colosseum   built in Rome in the first century AD. A building open to the sky with a large area where fights took place between gladiators and wild animals. Races and mock naval battles were also shown there
convent   a place where women, usually nuns, live together in a religious community

damask   woven patterned silk, originally made in Damascus, Syria
Decameron   a book written by the Italian author Boccaccio in which ten people are staying in a villa outside Florence to avoid the plague. Each tells a story every day for ten days, making one hundred stories in all
diptych   a picture consisting of two parts usually hinged together like the pages of a book. There are often paintings on all four surfaces
dissection   cutting up and investigating a dead body
Doge   the chief law-keeper and ruler of Italian states like Venice and Genoa
dowry   money or goods given by a woman's father to the man she marries

fable   a story not based on fact, often with animals as characters
Flanders   the area of modern-day Belgium
fresco   a painting done on wet plaster on a wall or ceiling

guild   a society of people who do the same work, trade or craft. In Florence employers and workers belonged to the same guild

hose   usually stockings worn by men and women. Men's hose often had leather soles on the feet

lute   stringed instrument like a guitar, but with a rounded body

manuscript   a book written by hand
Mass   important service in the Roman Catholic Church where communion is taken
millet   seed of a plant used for food
mural   a wall painting

Netherlands   the area of modern-day Belgium and Holland

orbit   the path a planet takes around the Sun, or moons around a planet

Pantheon   a temple, built in Rome in the second century AD, which was converted into a church in the seventh century AD and was therefore a Roman building which had not become a ruin
patron   someone who pays an artist to work for him or her
pendulum   a weight suspended so that it is free to swing. In clocks it is a weighted rod which can be raised or lowered to make the clock accurate
perspective   a way of drawing or painting to create a feeling of space and distance in a picture, making things look three-dimensional on a two-dimensional surface
pilgrimage   a visit to a saint's tomb or shrine or other holy place
post-mortem   cutting into and investigation of a dead body, often to find out the cause of death
pumice stone   stone formed when the lava erupting from a volcano cools; used for rubbing things smooth

secular   non-religious
sfumato   gradual, smoke-like shading used in painting to avoid harsh lines
siege   when an army surrounds the walls of a city or castle waiting for the people inside to surrender. War machines were used to try to break down the walls or force the people out
sinew   tough, fine tissue which joins the muscle to the bone
spa   place where there is a pool or spring of water containing mineral salts, which is said to have healing properties
swaddled   way of wrapping new-born babies tightly in layers of sheets

tendons   a strong band of tissue at the end of a muscle where it is fixed to the bone
typeface   the kind of lettering used to compose a page of printed writing

urban (urbanised)   where there are many houses, shops, businesses, etc. (people living in cities rather than in the countryside)

vault   an arched ceiling or roof
villa   large house or mansion built in the classical style

woodcut   print made by carving a picture or a design on wood, spreading it with ink and pressing it on to paper

Index

Agony and the Ecstasy, The (Stone) 28–9
Aldine Press 58
anatomy 42–5
Anguissola, Sofonisba 38–9
architecture 32–5
astronomy 46–9

Bacon, Roger 8
Belgium *see* Flanders
Black Death *see* plague
block printing 55
Boccaccio 40
Brahe, Tycho 46
Breugel, Pieter the Elder 50–1
Brunelleschi, Filippo 35

Church 8, 12
    views on astronomy 47
    views on medicine 8, 43
city states 10
classical civilisation 8, 12–13
    architecture 32
    art 24
    astronomy 46
    medicine 42
clocks, pendulum 48–9
Copernicus, Nicolaus 46, 47

Datini, Francesco di Marco 36, 38, 41
Datini, Margherita 38, 41, 42
Decameron (Boccaccio) 40
doctors 41–2
Duke of Milan 16

Este, Isabella d' 38

Fabric of the Human Body, The (Vesalius) 44, 45
Flanders (now Belgium) 50

Florence 10–11, 32–5
    health and medicine 40–2
    Leonardo in Florence 14–15
Florence Cathedral (Duomo, Santa Maria del Fiore) 34, 35

Galen, Claudius 42–3
Galileo Galilei 47–9
Government Square (Piazza della Signoria), Florence 34
Greek civilisation *see* classical civilisation
Gutenberg, Johann 56

health 40–5
Hoby, Thomas 32–5
hospitals 42

Italy 10–13, 60–1

Kepler, Johann 46–7

law of falling bodies 48
Leonardo da Vinci 14–21
Lives of the Artists (Vasari) 20–1, 39

marriage 37–8
Medici, Cosimo de' 36
Medici, Lorenzo de' 11, 37, 42–3
Medici family 11, 15
medicine 40–5
Michelangelo 28–9
Middle Ages 6
    architecture 32
    art 22–3
    astrology 46
    books 54
    medicine 42–3
Milan 16

Newton, Isaac 48
Northern Europe 50–3

paper-making 55
patrons 15
    women 38
pendulums 48–9
Philip of Spain 39
Piazza della Signoria (Government Square), Florence 34
plague 40–1
Ponte Vecchio (Old Bridge), Florence 33
portrait painting 30–1
printing 54–9

religion
    religious art 22–3, 25–7
    see also Church
Roman civilisation *see* classical civilisation
Roman Empire 8, 12–13

Santa Maria del Fiore (Cathedral, Duomo), Florence 34, 35
Sistine Chapel, Rome 28–9
slavery 36
Stone, Irving 28–9

towns 12
Tsai Lun 55

van Eyck, Jan 53
van Heemskerck, Marten 50
Vasari, Giorgio 20–1, 39
Verrocchio, Andrea del 14
Vesalius, Andreas 44–5

warfare 12
women's role 36–9